A

Veteran in

Voice and Verse

by

Mark Lanchbery

Third Uncut Edition June 2021

Cover photograph: The Rift Valley

1

07885 414549

Foreword

I have faced many challenges in my life some good, some bad

I have hurt and loved many people made some laugh, and some sad

But never in my life have I wanted to see people maimed, hurt or die

In the guise of some cause when the only question I'm left with is why?

I live my life wondering if I could have done things different you see

To make me a better person, to be kinder to the people who love me

But life isn't like that, we all have our flaws to live with and bear

So I have learnt to surround myself with people who matter and care

If you are one of these people then please accept my apologies sincere

But also accept my thank you and love for being my rock and here.

Dedicated to:

My long suffering family, my brothers in arms and friends, my amazing and loyal companion Jerry who all; through the years through no fault of their own have had to live with my PTSD and physical injuries, without you all playing your part I would not be the person I am today and for that I thank you all.

Also:

The dedication and support of the people that I cannot mention in this book for various reasons; you are not forgotten.

Part One

'The Voice'

The COVID Catastrophe

And other Rants!

Table of Contents 1:

****

Table of Contents 2:

****

A Beautiful Day

20th March 2020

Today was a beautiful day to wake up, the sun was shining and all was right with the world when I looked out of my window towards the Bowling Green.

Jerry was making himself known to me for his daily walk and sniff about in the woods at the back of my house, he normally runs up and down the stairs flying around until I get dressed which takes time as I suffer from disabilities gained whilst on active service with the British Army in 2008.

Today was also shopping day, something I always dread, especially in the current climate of a new disease sweeping the planet which was supposed to have symptoms of colds and influenza?

On the 16th of March Boris Johnson our Prime Minister had warned everybody in the country to be aware of the disease and keep away from other people as much as possible, the jokes were coming in thick and thin regarding the name of this disease 'Corona' I bet in hindsight people now would not be so quick to take the piss out of this virus!

Corona bottled lager came in for a lot of rib tickling and was just about the only lager left on the shelves in the supermarkets!

Despite the warnings and some peoples paranoia life went on as much as usual, people still went to work, people still went to the beach, people still went to the pub and I still went to the gym, a very important thing for me as I use light exercise on non impact machines to relieve some of my symptoms from pain, this works well in conjunction with the morphine I have to take on a daily basis, this helps me lead some sort of life, after being injured in 2008 I have to admit life has been tough, everything is a struggle for me from getting dressed to having a shower to cooking a meal, apart from the pain I have restricted movement in my arms, back, legs and neck.

Jerry has been trained as an Assistance Dog and he helps me with certain tasks such as loading and unloading the washing machine, picking things up from the floor, waking me up from persistent nightmares due to my PTSD and reminding me to take my medication by bringing me the medication pouch and depositing it in my lap.

After dressing, making myself a boiled egg and running Jerry around the block it was time to get myself into the car and head for the local supermarket to do the weekly shopping, sometimes even this task is to much for me and I am lucky to have a great network of friends who will help me and do the shopping if I ask them.

Walking around the aisles I noticed that the shelves were getting empty? Things like toilet rolls, hand sanitizer and pasta!

I mentioned this to another shopper in the extensive queue waiting to get to the check out and he showed me a video on his phone of a massive crowd in Leighton London outside of a supermarket waiting for it to open and the mayhem when the doors eventually let people in!

At this point in time we had not been told to avoid people or not to stand close to them in queues so I didn't think to keep my distance, but I do remember thinking to myself at that moment; talking to this mystery shopper that he didn't look very well, he looked like he had a cold or bad hay fever, little did I know that this was probably the time when I contracted a killer disease that we now know to be COVID 19 and my journey into hell was about to begin and take me through another time in my life when I thought I was going to die, not with bullets and bombs this time but with a silent, deadly, invisible, unrelenting, powerful and dangerous enemy, one that if you show no respect, trust to luck rather than judgement will find its way in and take your life.

****

Why Toilet Rolls?

So why toilet rolls? Was it the power of Face book, the power of suggestion, or just downright stupidity and sheeples syndrome?

The answer will probably never be known, one of those things that will disappear into the ethers of time because nobody wants to put their hand up and take ownership of being an absolute spunk trumpet.

If you were writing a doomsday book and you had a paragraph within telling how people would be fighting in the aisles of a supermarket to get the last packet of toilet rolls it would drop into the realms of fantasy, you can never have too many toilet rolls in a pandemic, they are bound to come in useful for all sorts of things, like... well like... well you know...

I have had the opportunity to ask the question on a few occasions and one drop's into my mind almost immediately of a day in a supermarket watching a shopper well into his 60s try and put 10 packs of 9 toilet rolls into his trolley; it was like watching an episode of the Krypton Factor or The Cube in real life, I expected the Gordon the Gopher bloke to jump out at any minute, but of course he didn't, this was real, in real-time in the middle of a supermarket aisle ☺ this guy was trying to fit 90 toilet rolls in a trolley, I watched half amused and half disbelieving; eventually he saw me watching and smiled, this was my cue to ask in a polite and constructive way 'why do you need all those rolls mate' he replied 'the wife asked me to come down and get as many as I could' not really thinking that was an answer I said 'but why? What is she going to do with them?' he thought about this for a moment with a blank expression on his face and then just shrugged!

I am guessing this is the power of suggestion and a good woman, for a man to go out and blindly buy 90 toilet rolls without question is blinding obedience and he probably has a very happy marriage.

I; on the other hand have never been able to keep my mouth shut and blindly follow orders; testament to my numerous failed relationships and always getting a smack around the ear when I was a kid for saying 'but why?'

I'm guessing the same as we have herd immunity what we have here is a case of herd mentality; the same people for instance who always bought a Ford Escort because their mates had one, then bought a Ford Sierra because their mates had one, then a Ford Granada because their mates had one, these people didn't want to stand out from the crowd, just to be 'one of the boys' didn't want to be different, sticking with the pack, the grey man, never attracting attention to one's self, and now they buy toilet rolls because everyone else is buying toilet rolls, they don't know why so they just shrug instead of questioning, they really cannot help themselves, it's how they have always survived in the past, how they have got along, how they gained and kept their mates, how they won promotion at work, how they got invited to all the best parties.

Me; no I didn't buy masses of toilet roll and I have never yet run out, I never had a Ford of any description, choosing instead to be different and choose Alfa Romeo and Saab, never had many mates but the ones I did have were worth having and absolutely priceless to me, mates I trusted with my life and never regretted it.

Oh! And as for parties I've been described as the original social hand grenade if you get bored and want things livened up, just pull out the pin, and then roll me across the dance floor and **Stand and Stare** ☺

****

Why Toilet Rolls Part II

So today is Sunday 27th September 2020 and we are not in lockdown there is no shortage of food, pasta, bread, milk or any other commodities BUT!

Toilet Rolls are all gone from the shelves yet again, what in the name of all that is holy is happening; yet again the mobs are out there, the spineless moronic cretins are buying up all the toilet rolls!

These are probably the same people who did it last time the selfish, ignorant people, who spark panic and fear, the same people who look you in the eye and complain that they cannot find any toilet rolls and they have run out whilst you being the good neighbour you are lend them some of yours which they squirrel away smugly knowing they have got a few more rolls to hoard away, the same people who with no thought for anybody else go into the local supermarket time and time again buying one pack at a time because the store has rationed everyone to one pack each.

I have sat in the car park of my local store and seen these people who leave their stupid dumb (don't say boo to a goose, just nod and smile☺) husbands in the car (just in case they need to make a quick getaway) whilst they go into the store to grab another pack of toilet rolls, again and again around and around they go like ants bringing food back to the nest, triumphant at every new pack they bring out, no guilt, no shame just pure greed.

What a sad reflection on society that some of us behave in this manner, who told anybody that there was going to be a shortage of toilet rolls in the first place, was this just posh mums school gate gossip, standing there refreshed from their Pilates class, Costa Coffee in one hand and mobile phone in the other so they can keep abreast no doubt who has stocks of toilet roll and where ☺

Maybe it was in the papers and I didn't see it, maybe it was on the news, maybe even it was because one of the mums went round for a coffee morning and saw a toilet roll mountain in her neighbour's garage and suddenly got that dreaded of all feelings the FOMO (fear of missing out) maybe they had

17

nothing better to do during the day so it was some sort of new game, maybe they need the toilet rolls for some impending national emergency that has somehow passed my attention who knows?

All I do know is some of the people of my village have **NOT** moved on since the last time they bought all the toilet rolls they are still selfish, hoarding bastards, but I did see some of my neighbours with their stockpiles last time and there they are again buying yet more, which means in six months they must have got through a massive amount of toilet rolls which leads me to the conclusion that not only do they talk a load of shit and spread a lot of shit but they must also do a lot of shit ☺

Is any chance of borrowing a toilet roll anyone? **NO** I thought not ☺

****

Supermarket Sweep!

What has happened to the Supermarkets? Why did they allow the public to completely strip the shelves?

One would like to think that they just got caught 'off guard' or could it have been a bit of 'profiteering'?

Taking advantage of the 'panic' of the public during a rising pandemic, allowing people to fill their trolleys to overflowing as long as they could pay for it!

Having a total disregard for old people, disabled people, people relying on benefits, nurses, shift workers, as long as the tills were ringing they didn't care, the shelves were emptied within minutes, they hired more staff to fill the shelves, are these staff still employed now? I doubt it, you just had the thought walking around; that the supermarket kept the shelves semi empty so people would buy more, kept some back in the store room so they could trickle out the goods so people would think there was a shortage, putting goods with higher prices on the shelves rather than the cheaper version to make more profit, but they wouldn't do that would they?

This went on for weeks and weeks before the public started to realise they were on a bit of a ride, the emergency nurse who had finished her shift and couldn't buy any food because the wonderful public who may have had to rely on that nurse were stripping the shelves bare in a manic lust of senseless and selfish greed.

People's behaviour was embarrassing; I fought for people who were a bloody embarrassment I was ashamed of what the so called British people had become!

Those words spoken by that nurse pulled the supermarkets up sharp they were at risk of being caught out for profiteering and not protecting the people that they were there to actually serve, I suggest they gripped the situation just in time before the public took matters into their own hands!

The Cambridge Dictionary definition of profiteering is:

Profiteering is the act of taking advantage of a situation in order to make a profit, usually by charging high prices for things people need.

Does this ring any bells? at your local shop or supermarket? Hand Gel, Toilet Rolls, Pasta, Tinned Food, Alcohol, this list goes on and on, as I suggested before; the supermarkets turned their profiteering around just in time and now they have introduced 'social distancing' rationing of some products and put on a happy smiling face when they allow you 'the customer' to shop in 'their' store using 'their' rules no wonder they are smiling.

When this is all over questions will be asked and I'm sure some loyalties will be changed and challenged, I'm not even going to start to write about catching COVID in your store because you failed miserably to bring in social distancing in time; in your rush putting 'profits before people'

****

The Hoarders

After clearing the supermarket shelves of everything and anything where did the hoarders store their booty?

Well I can say where one of my close neighbours stored theirs because I had the pleasure of watching these hoarding bastards, these doomsday preppers, these selfish pull the ladder up jack I'm ok people store it away.

These are professional people the husband; well he works in London most of the week and the wife works in a local school so you would think that these were rational people, a fine upstanding pillar of our community, somebody to look up to and admire.

Well I watched this guy take his precious sports car out of the garage to make way for a 3rd large freezer in which to store his hoarded goods from the supermarket, the sports car is his pride and joy, he is always out there polishing and tinkering with it; in normal circumstances he would have never even dreamed of leaving it outside to get dusty or wet, but sure enough there it was parked up on his drive to make way for the food he was going to store away for his impending holocaust.

Three large freezers full of food; and floor to ceiling tins, bottled water and you guessed it toilet rolls, and yet everyday I saw his wife go out in her little car first thing in the morning and come back with more, more tins more bottled water, more toilet roll, it was never ending, the selfishness of these people because they had more money then anyone else was outstanding even for me to watch, I have been to some really poor places around the world where people have nothing, no food, no clean water to drink and more often then not only the clothes they stand in, even in this country there are poor people, people that shop from one day or week to the next because they havent got the money to load up their cupboards with food for a 'rainy day'

What these so called professional people were doing was unforgivable; them and the people like them were causing misery to our village, old people, people on the front line working, people that didnt have much were being 'robbed' yes I say robbed because this is what these people were doing robbing the more unfortunate than themselves to hoard food and other supplies in their garage, do you think they would be ashamed? I doubt it otherwise would they be doing it? I want to challenge them, let people know they are living next door to selfish, robbing bastards! But would that help? Would it do any good or should I be doing the same thing? All these questions go through your mind tying up your thoughts whilst you are trying to steer your way through the COVID illness.

In the end I left sleeping dogs to lie until I was strong enough to be able to take on these thoughts and concerns and now I am writing it down to cleanse my system to deplete my anger, yes they are; despite their obvious intelligence; scumbags, but what can anyone do if some people want to act in this way, to have disregard and disrespect for their fellow man, to instead of pulling together and looking out for people for the common good they hoard, deprive other people of their fair share, squirrel their food away in their garage and can still look their neighbours and people in the eye and pretend that they are still the pillars of the community.

Well I know what you are and you leave a bitter taste in my mouth, but there are unfortunatley millions in this country like you, it is a scourge of our society that it times of need people like you will revert to your real character, that of a dangerous wild animal willing to take and kill if neccessary to protect your selfish selves; so take a bow hoarding neighbours and pray I'm not there waiting when you look back up!.

****

Lockdown

Another very 'un' British word borrowed from our American cousins with all the others such as; 'like' and 'so' and now we have 'lockdown' to add to the death of the English language.

So what does 'Lockdown' actually mean according to the free dictionary?

A protocol followed in an emergency that involves confining people in a secure place, such as the confinement of prison inmates in cells after a disturbance, or the locking in of students and teachers in classrooms after a violent attack.

So now I hope that's cleared that up for everybody, as I am neither a prisoner in an American jail or long past being a student WTF has it got to do with me?

It has nothing at all to do with not going out or closing down shops it is a word that sounds sinister, it sounds right out there, it's a word used by the trendy people, the with it brigade and Muppets who think that in Great Britain in 2020 they are living in the American 'hood' ☺

The media love it; it's a trendy word it rolls off the broadcasters tongue like a knob of butter off a hot knife.

You are on lockdown BUT you can go to work, you are on lockdown BUT you can go out shopping, you are on lockdown BUT you can go outside for exercise, you are on lockdown BUT you can do anything you bloody like really, BUT you must not break the cardinal rule of lockdown and that's getting caught by a policeman whose job it is to decide whether you are breaking any of these lockdown rules even though he only saw you 10 minutes ago unless you speak to him in an American accent and live in the 'hood'

I expect real American prisoners are spinning in their cells hearing the incorrect use of their word being used all over the British media for them the term lockdown means the complete opposite, definitely NOT going out anytime soon, definitely NOT going shopping, definitely NOT getting much exercise.

The only lockdown I've ever come across was the lockdown sung about by the band 'Blue' in the song 'Fly By' so even I am perplexed as to what lockdown actually means in the sense we are using it but I will persevere and try!

Lockdown means stay at home as much as possible and limit your contact with other people, easy for me as I'm not very sociable anyway (see odd people) ☺ only go out to get essential stuff, hair colouring or pot plants do not count as essential (sorry)

By essential they mean bread, water, food, milk, medicines, medical help, not lets go to the beach and have a BBQ or a 70 mile bike ride in the countryside riding 4 abreast slowing down someone delivering essential medical supplies or medicines in their car for people staying in because you think these volunteer responders shouldn't be driving on **your** road; the road that **you** pay no insurance to drive on or no road tax to repair; lockdown means doing all these sensible things and taking all sensible precautions to keep you and your family safe, safe from getting at the very least ill and at the very worst dying or even worse still making someone else close to you die!

But here I am again trying to explain; and if I hear myself trying to explain you are **NOT** going to understand **ARE YOU?**

****

Social Distancing

Social Distancing to most is a very complicated thing; I would like to go all Freud on you, but in the case of Joe Public it would just be a load of old bullocks.

Humans naturally gravitate to each other it is what has kept mankind alive since time has begun, but in the case of some of the public and in today's current climate some find it impossible to switch that part of their 'brain' off!

The Government introduced social distancing to keep us safe, safe from contracting a deadly virus, safe from passing it on to others and safe from dying, this is known as survival, another basic requirement of life that has kept humans from dying out.

If the Government had said you must do social distancing for your survival people may have listened, for some of the public things have to be spelt out and enforced, the only thing they understand is being told in no uncertain terms what to do.

Short of telling them what to do some people are going to struggle with any concept.

This is why when you join any of the services they start breaking you down from day 1 to a base level, it doesn't matter where you were before; you are broken down (or some are just broken☺) and then when you are at rock bottom they start to build you up again to the services way of thinking; so everyone understands, everyone is singing from the same song sheet, there can be NO excuses, no 'I didn't know sir'!

And then there is Joe Public, with some who think they always know better, think they have a right to add something, think they are cleverer and more intelligent then the next man, so when you tell them something they think to themselves 'I know better' this is because no one has broken them down; maybe when they were children nobody gave them a slap and told them to

Behave and be quiet, to just do as they were told, unfortunately for the rest of us this behaviour has carried them through their lives without consequence

So to tell them they have to social distance whether it be in a supermarket, out on a walk, in the street or heading into your space, these people neither understand, want to understand or care, which is why; when you politely tell them to keep their distance they give you that blank/hurt look as if to say why do I have to keep my distance, I know better then you even if you maybe an eminent pandemic virologist.

These people have never ever done as they were told, maybe their parents never told them, and in any case they are never going to change now, maybe getting a little slap or told off for doing something naughty when they were younger would have saved them from getting an even bigger slap now from a deadly virus and dying for not keeping their distance!

****

PPE

Where is all the PPE? Well I can give you my opinion, we have not got any!

The Government despite telling everyone who could be bothered to listen it was spending millions on PPE they were absolutely NOT.

They were too busy hoping all this would 'go away' and cure itself before anyone not only noticed but got sick.

They sent soldiers to Iraq with weapons that didn't work, a criminal shortage of ammunition, armoured Land Rovers that had no protection for the occupants against an IED and body armour that was out of date and hard to come by.

In short we had to fight a war with hardly any ammunition and minimal PPE in the hope that it would all be over soon and we could head for home a tea and medals without having to spend any real money.

This literally blew up in the Governments faces years later when they had to pay out compensation for the deaths and injuries caused by lack of proper armour in our 'armoured' Land Rovers (snatch) so memories are short in Great Britain, most of the great British public remember nothing of the fighting we did in some far away land to keep them safe with no PPE!

And fast forward to a few years later and here we are again, the NHS is crying out for PPE in a war of their own against a killer virus, being sent into the front line with no protection, no armour, and no ammunition, sounds familiar doesn't it?

The Government yet again trying to do everything on the cheap, yet again, trying to keep the costs down and hope beyond all hope that the virus just 'goes away'

All the promises and rhetoric sounded great; almost plausible but the reality once again was many moons away, complete and utter bollocks and fantasy, I would love to have been in on the meetings that went before the daily

Briefing if indeed they even had one! Judging by the Government Ministers and so called experts that crawl out from the woodwork everyday to talk more utter bollocks to a nation craving for news and in fear, I find it very hard to believe that they talked about anything before they went out to face the public.

STAY AT HOME – SAVE THE NHS- SAVE LIVES

STAY AT HOME;

Unless you are a Government Minister/Advisor or Scientist wanting a shag!

SAVE THE NHS;

Unless it's going to cost us; the Government a few quid in PPE

SAVE LIVES;

Unless you're a country that's got the biggest death toll in Europe

And then we find out the Government have shelled out millions of pounds on buying PPE from Turkey and it is absolutely useless for use in hospitals or care homes, but will the procurement officer be sacked?

I take you back to the useless equipment the Government gave us soldiers to go and fight a real war, with real bullets and real bombs, **NOTHING** learnt here then! ☺

****

The Surgery

During my illness certain things stood out at my local surgery mostly to do with the treatment I received.

Several times I attended the surgery and was examined, but nothing seemed to stand out for them to give a proper diagnosis; I had breathing problems, shortness of breath, tightness in the chest, pain in chest and lungs every time I took breath in, but it always seemed to me despite examinations nobody really want to commit to a diagnosis.

You almost had a feeling they knew what the problem 'could' be and didn't want to say, indeed one of the team said 'there is nothing I can give you it would be better if you just went home and tried to get over it' but get over what exactly?

I think the NHS knew what was coming concerning the Corona Virus but for whatever reason wanted to keep things quiet and well under the radar.

I did have some absolutely superb treatment and care from various sources, an ECG which showed my heart was fine and some basic blood tests early on in my illness which came back clear but still no test for the obvious thing, I was then prescribed some anti-inflammatory drugs which did seem to help in a small way, but although they took away the pain I still had the shortness of breath and feeling very unwell.

From there on in things got progressively worse, headaches, sore throat, dry cough, sweating, nausea, extreme tiredness, sleeping badly at night but the one thing that was strange was my temperature, always between 34.2 and 36.4 I started to do my own observations everyday taking my temperature, pulse and blood pressure and recording them along with my daily symptoms.

At night my breathing seemed extremely poor and several nights I woke up gasping for breath and trying to remain calm whilst getting some oxygen into my lungs, it can only be described as feeling like you were drowning, there

Were several nights through the worst of it that I really thought that I would never see the morning, my family or Jerry again?

Through several of the nights I woke up and found Jerry actually in the bed cuddled into me 'Jerry NEVER' gets in the bed, but there he was pushing himself right into me, being there when I woke up, sometimes licking my face and neck to wake me up.

I went to the surgery again one more time and had an extensive round of blood tests; again the surgery staff were amazing, the bloods were sent off and again all came back clear, so why was I still so unwell? And again nobody wanted to say those dreaded words, but my logic being if I had been tested for everything else and it wasn't that; it only left one thing!

****

Written March 2020

The Government

Let's bury our heads in the sand and hope it all goes away!

This was definitely the mantra of the day for quite a long period of time; the Government knew what was coming; but I'm sure under extreme pressure from the public and media letting massive concerts and meetings go ahead such as Cheltenham and various rock concerts this turned out to be absolute folly! But in the good old British way we kept calm and carried on and got infected! But this was something the 'stiff upper lip' was never going to beat.

The failure on the part of the Government to lock things down and put a plan in place to keep people informed and safe so they could make their own minds up has undoubtedly caused deaths.

One could be kind and say that nobody could have envisaged the problems and the strength of the virus; and they could have an argument to that end, but the warning signs were there as early as November 2019, but these were ignored at the very best and downright lies and deceit at the worst.

But I'm going to be kind and hang around in the middle of the argument for a bit; we continued to allow flights and foreigners into our island fortress even from China; we continued to bring back people who were infected and let them disappear into the populace, we continued to allow people to socialise with each other even though it was going to cause more infection and ultimately deaths why?

Herd immunity! Better to let everyone get the virus, build up some immunity to it; then we can all get on with our lives, but herd immunity is OK if you are dealing with measles, mumps, the common cold, flu, chicken pox but surely not a virus that attacks the respiratory system in people and kills some of them; herd immunity is great when you have a fair idea of the inception and run of the germ or virus, not when we are dealing with something that is completely new and know nothing about, using humans as guinea pigs in a massive world laboratory is almost bordering on the criminally insane; like

Something from the Nazi concentration camps of years past, it seems some of us still haven't learnt from those lessons.

And then we have the daily briefings; the; we cannot do anything now it's all too late so we will revert back to plan 'A'.

Bullshit Baffles Brains; something that was taught and drummed into us in the British Army when we first joined up, to be fair to the Government the last thing people need when they are trying to grasp the realities of lockdown, empty supermarkets and furlough is to be told bullshit!

The Government needed something to distract, and quickly, so they picked on the one thing that the British Public wouldn't question or rise up against, they had already used wounded service personnel, ethnic minorities, now they needed something else, a quick look around, delve into the box and what pops up? You guessed it the NHS, I always wondered why they bang on and on about the NHS, it could be to give the public something to do, something to raise money for, something to believe in again, a tool to be used to deflect incoming flak away from the Government, we love our NHS dearly so we would be less likely to rock the boat and ask awkward questions, when the Government are asked awkward questions next time you watch a daily briefing watch them trawl out the NHS like it's some sort of magic wand!

The truth maybe ugly, the truth may hurt and sometimes the truth is a downright 'bastard' but we can take it; we are British and we are proud.

Remember, it would be good for you to look back on this and think to yourselves; did the Government do all it could to protect us and look after us?

Or do you get the feeling that we have all been royally shafted yet again?

****

Testing

A certain Government Minister promised us faithfully to get testing for the corona virus up to 100,000 tests per day by the end of April; he was a little economical with the truth and failed!

Not only did he fail he tried to pull the wool over the eyes of the British public and doctored the figures at the last minute to make it look like he had achieved his goal, nobody batted an eyelid! Why?

Why is this cheating Government Minister still in office, we cannot believe a word he says, surely integrity should be the mainstay of being in Government office or at least an attempt at a tiny bit of integrity, but we have seen this before; we have had a long run of Government Ministers and Prime Ministers who shall we say have had questionable integrity, I'm hoping I don't have to start reeling out the names (Blair) and yet they continue to hoodwink the public and the public 'suck it up' they never challenge what is being said or ask questions that will 'rock the boat'

So what exactly are these tests? Do they work? If you ask the question nobody seems to know, when I had my blood tests for literally everything, liver function, kidney function, white blood cells, red blood cells, diabetes, thyroid, inflammatory markers etc but not one single hint of a test for covid, why?

When I challenged this; the nurses taking the blood just looked at each other and said nothing, was there a 'real' test? Or is it just another Government smoke screen a red herring to keep us all occupied.

Was the so called test just a placebo, my blood tests all came back negative so if by their own testing I was in perfect health why was I living an absolute month of hell being so unwell, fighting every day to get back to some sort of health with all the symptoms of covid.

If indeed there was an actual test why wasn't I tested for the most obvious thing? The Government were trying to reach their 100,000 test goal yet were not testing people who showed clear and actual signs of the disease.

Did the Government try hard enough to get people tested with a test that actually worked, a test that would make a difference, I suggest not!

I have now the definitive answer, there were no real tests, the Government are not even testing staff within the NHS because there is no reliable test and if staff were tested positive there would be such a shortage of staff the NHS would collapse.

So there we have it; we have been deceived and lied to yet again in the hope the British public will believe everything that they are told and the virus will just please 'go away' ☺

****

Written April 2020

Conspiracy Theories

One has to wonder what is happening here. How could it be possible that sober, intelligent people all-over the world have suddenly lost their capacity to think, question, analyse and even do simple mathematics.

The same people praising the government now were, just a few weeks ago before the lockdown, still moaning and groaning about how useless and corrupt their government is.
Strange how those corrupt fools suddenly became praiseworthy angels from heaven. It confounds the mind. The corrupt, selfish, greedy fools are now being praised and commended for killing the economy that will leave MILLIONS jobless thanks to brainwashed sheeple - who never learned to question anything - screaming "We're all going to die".

By the time most people awaken from their coronaphobic trance, it will be too late, because all seven billion inhabitants of this planet could in future be force-vaccinated by Bill Gates, possibly along with a tracking implant that would also serve as an identification and certification of vaccination.

It does not really matter what happens from here onwards, because the powers that be have already achieved more than what is needed to finish what they began, which is to collapse, reset, the world economy, to equalise everyone, and make them dependent upon the state or upon the banks and big corporations that own and control the state. The world is now in a depression and it will be much, much worse than the great depression of 1929.

Welcome to the "new normal" under the New World Order and imminent One World Government probably to be headed by Bill the vaccine pusher at the Gates of hell, supported and praised for it by 80% of the world's zombified population.

So how did this happen?

It is not the facts and the realities of events or situations that dictate people's response and behaviour; it is people's perceptions of it that determines their reactions, behaviours and ultimately the outcome.

Whoever controls or manipulates those perceptions, controls and finally determines the outcome and of course, "Whoever controls the media, controls the mind." - Jim Morrison.

The expression "The big lie" actually originated from Adolf Hitler, when he dictated his 1925 book Mein Kampf, about the use of a lie so "colossal" that no one would believe that someone "could have the impudence to distort the truth so infamously".

It is claimed that Joseph Goebbels wrote the following: "If you tell a lie big enough and keep repeating it, people will eventually come to believe it. The lie can be maintained only for such time as the State can shield the people from the political, economic and/or military consequences of the lie. It thus becomes vitally important for the State to use all of its powers to repress dissent, for the truth is the mortal enemy of the lie, and thus by extension, the truth is the greatest enemy of the State."
Repetition is used widely in the media, advertising, politics and wherever persuasion is required, because by simply repeating a message or lie its persuasive effect is increased dramatically.

Research has proven that, the more we hear something, the more we believe it, the more validity we give to it and "unless contrary information is acquired", the more persuaded we are by it. Also, the easier the message is to understand the more it is adopted by the subconscious as truth, even when the person making the statement is lying. Psychologists call it - "the illusion of truth".

Once the lie becomes generally accepted (popular) public opinion, it develops a life of its own. Particularly if the lie contains an element of fear, any dissent is viewed as a threat to society. It at this point those not even highly respected are true experts on the subject, let alone political leaders, dare to express any opposing views on the entrenched narrative. The lie has now become the truth and actual truth gets labelled as dissent, even punishable by Law. "In a time of universal deceit, telling the truth is a revolutionary act." - George Orwell

Mainstream science is almost 100% dependent on funding and you cannot be funded and independent at the same time, "He who makes the rain controls the game" - Dan Lok. For the right amount of funding and personal gain, mainstream science can validate or invalidate and will support or oppose anything their funders demand.

The CIA made up the term, "Conspiracy Theorist" after the JFK assassination to discredit the "Truth Seekers" who said that what the public was told was nothing but a big lie.

The term "Conspiracy Theorist" has been "weaponised" to discredit anyone who questions any popular / public opinion or generally accepted narrative.

Particularly in politics, there is no such thing as coincidence, nothing happens spontaneously of by chance. Everything is well planned, organised and orchestrated. President Bush warned about a disease such as this, back in 2006 already, Bill the vaccine pusher at the Gates of hell warned about this back in 2015 already, Dr. Fauci predicted in 2017 that "a surprise outbreak of a massive disease would strike during this [the Trump] administration", and it was pre-empted by a Netflix movie called "Contagion" in 2019. Also remember the ID2020 simulated practice run in 2019.

If the purpose of "the big lie" is to create a distraction from something much bigger to be done behind the scenes, one needs to get rid of all other possible distractions, opposing views and suppress all opposing views.

So let us go back to Hitler and Goebbels and break this down:

First you need a massive scare, like a mysterious "unknown killer disease". Scenes get distributed of seemingly healthy asymptomatic people suddenly dying in the streets, scenes of dead people lying in buildings, streets, parks and all-over. They would not need to repeat this anywhere else, because they know that people would soon forget about the sudden death scare. Show how a large city is forced to bring in the military to lockdown everyone, welding the entrances and exits of buildings closed to imprison thousands of people inside, to prevent this "mysterious killer disease" from escaping and spreading.

Drive massive fear into people by telling them that 30 million people could die, 2.2-million people in America, 500,000 in the U.K., 150,000 in Australia and so forth.

Now get rid of any and all distractions. Sport is the all-time biggest, most passionate distraction in the world, so shut down sport immediately, because they need to retain everyone's focus on the "killer" distraction.

Repeat the message of the fearful distraction as often as possible, flood the media, including social media with it. Place a banner about the disease at the top of every webpage possible, at the top of every YouTube video, have it on radio and television all day long. Occupy their minds with it and do not let up. Occupy people's minds completely, to the exclusion of everything else. The only thing people should be focussed on should be the horrific, deadly, fearful "killer" distraction created by the elite.

Now block all possible dissent and opposing views by gagging all health care professionals, real scientists and true experts from expressing their educated views in public. Make it a punishable offense for them to do so. Videos are censored, removed, websites and channels get blocked and removed to block out any dissent or opposing views. The only narrative allowed should be the narrative created by the elite and the media they control. Further to this. the public should be allowed the freedom on social media to drive each other crazy with rumours, without any health professionals or experts intervening and setting the record straight.

Now turn them against each other, "Divide and Rule". Every right that we have ever lost was because of the unaffected citizens supporting and praising the government for stealing the rights of those affected by it. How do governments achieve this?

Their "Divide and Rule" strategy was perfected a long time ago, with the so-called "fight against tobacco". Most people actually believe the myth that the "fight against tobacco" is because their government cares about them and their health. It has nothing to do with your beloved government caring about you or your health. No one cares about you, because you are neither that important nor that valuable. The only values you have are the taxes you pay into their pockets so that they could enrich themselves with it and use the rest to control and enslave you even more. The only other possible value you have is as expendable cannon fodder in mandatory military conscription.

The truth is that tobacco and alcohol are the pharmaceutical industry's biggest competition by far, nothing competes in that respect.

After decades of failing to kill the tobacco industry, big pharma's marketing departments came up with a brilliant idea; turn the non-smokers against the smokers by telling them that second-hand tobacco smoke is more dangerous than actual smoking. By convincing non-smokers that second-hand tobacco smoke is more dangerous than actual smoking; even children were turned against their parents, because of their smoking habits. Suddenly your dad who smoked became your enemy, because he supposedly posed a dangerous threat to your precious life!

You cannot judge people for their behaviour under circumstances where they are made to believe that their lives are in imminent danger. A person whose life is in imminent danger has broad latitude to do what is necessary to save his own life. They created the threat and they offered the solution, the cure. What followed was that those unaffected by the right, the non-smokers, cheered, praised and supported governments in stealing the rights of smokers, to save and protect themselves from the threat to their own precious lives.

The same tactic has since been deployed in every other "battle". In the fight against the right to own and bear firearms, the legal gun-owners are painted as being a danger and a threat to those who do not own firearms. In South Africa, those who do not own property support the government in confiscating the properties of those who legally own property, because property owners are painted as land thieves and rich criminals.

While non-smokers praised government to steal the rights of smokers, they sang another tune when the same government came for their guns, because now they themselves were affected. When those who praised government for stealing the rights of smokers and gun owners were themselves faced by government wanting to steal their properties, they became the affected. So every right every right ever lost was because of the unaffected supporting the government against the affected and in every case the government gained more power and the citizens lost more rights.

The cause of most human suffering is not "attachment" as Buddha suggested, but "self-pity". Because of their self-pity, people have become so accustomed to giving away personal rights in the face of any perceived threat to their own lives, "We're all going to die", that when their governments came with lockdowns they immediately agreed to it and those who do not abide by the lockdown rules, those who dissent and offer educated opposing views, are viewed as a dangerous threat to their own safety. Like Hitler repeatedly said, the government is doing it, because "It is for your own safety"....

In the meantime the distraction also offers opportunities for other agendas. Former White House Chief of Staff and Chicago Mayor, Rahm Emanuel (also known as known as Barack Obama's "get shit done" guy), famously said: "Never let a good crisis go to waste." Observe what is happening.
China and their partners are using this opportunity to buy countries, buy businesses, including mines and mineral rich land, at bargain prices. By the time this is all-over, if ever, China will own most of the current privately owned businesses and properties, all while we were being distracted...

****

By kind permission of Darren ☺

The BBC

The BBC is the so called stalwart of past and present broadcasting; the backbone of the nation; the place where everyone gets an up to date, unbiased, totally believable and truthful news story.

Bollocks!

This may have been true in World War Two; jutting out the stiff upper lip of Britain, broadcasting secret messages to our brave secret agents in enemy occupied territory; but wake up BBC those days are gone, the public is a more news savvy and intelligent breed nowadays and have a thirst for decent and unbiased news, not the clap trap you pour out every day over the airwaves in the guise of newsworthiness.

You are no longer broadcasting great speeches from Churchill to stir the nation into action, you are broadcasting complete and utter biased drivel; and unashamedly so; it's almost like you believe your own hype, your own 'spin' your own stories, if there are no stories you make them up or spin them out so thin a blind beggar could see the cracks.

You broadcast Government bullshit like your lives depended on it, everyday on your corona virus updates you allow half truths, some downright fiction, and Government Ministers to spout unbelievable figures and fill in with rubbish and now the cracks are beginning to show, the paper is falling off the walls as the glue melts, you are part of the Government rip off, the absolute travesty of the truth; everyday you allow Government Ministers to crawl out from their rocks and try to fool and deceive us with half truth figures, that do not stand up to even the slightest hint of inspection.

It is no wonder then that the British Public TV licence payers will continue to be ripped off for a few more years yet with the Government in your pocket.

Every morning you chuck out the same team to take the floor and soak us in your very twee, unashamed biased junk, it has got so bad that I think even the team start to believe the brainwashing drivel, they stare at the autocue

And sometimes almost squirm in embarrassment at the rhetoric they have to spiel out in the name of broadcasting.

Not one of the team challenges anyone, choosing instead to remain very polite and reserved such is the BBC way, frightened to upset any guest especially from the Government, the ruling classes, the ever so twee, and the middle class wannabe's.

Your cut glass accents and your PC rhetoric know no bounds, you have made this pandemic worse by delivering and broadcasting half truths and rhetoric to the general public, it would be interesting to see your viewing figures over this emergency compared to last year, maybe you should publicise them 'after doctoring the figures' for the viewers obviously.

All this said I would like to point out that I really do enjoy your Country File program on a Sunday evening, keep up the good work! ☺

UPDATE May 2021

It was always going to happen eventually; and it came in the guise of a serious backlash with the Princess Diana interviews carried out by reporter with a serious problem with seeing the truth obviously through his beer bottle glasses the truth became somewhat distorted at its best or downright blatant lies at its worse! At the moment the row carries on with the BBC trying to defend the indefensible and again sweep this under the carpet; just as they have done for many years; remember JS? Another time when the truth was there but the BBC done nothing but cover it up leaving more kids to suffer for longer at the hands of a person who thought he was untouchable because of the BBC ineptitude and inability to see and act on the truth; perhaps now they will lose their licence fee perhaps now they will realise that to Broadcast Bollocks Constantly is coming back to bite them.

****

42

Piers Morgan has left the building!

Piers Morgan has always been a controversial figure within the broadcasting community; his forthright and opinionated rhetoric has been the source of much amusement to me every morning for years.

This is a man who is either loved or hated; dividing Great Britain in the morning with his opinion polls and some say harsh treatment of particular government ministers, personally I think the government deserved everything they got; expecting us to believe the drivel they spouted on other channels and not dare to question anything.

Enter Piers Morgan; the only voice of reason and constructive argument we had left; now I am not saying the opinions of the great Piers were always right but one thing he did do was make you question yourself and more importantly question what the powers that be were doing to this great nation.

It was only a matter of time then that the motor mouth of ITV would fall flat on his arse one day and have to fall on his sword and resign but for such a feeble and pointless reason?

The drama show that was the interview with Oprah needed to be uncovered for what it was; American drivel television at its best (or worst) the young lady in question wanted us to believe that she was being bullied and feeling like she wanted to end things; that is her right she can feel what she wants but to air the dirty washing on television and add more drama then a Poldark series was unforgivable, we in this country have a stiff upper lip not the quivering bottom lips of an American drama queen seeking, nay craving and wanting more attention then she obviously gets by being married to one of our very own stoic and upstanding finest British men.

And then to add even more insult to injury a jumped up weather man hoisted himself into public orbit by jumping on the charabanc and used mock indignation to take down a fellow broadcaster; he used airtime to row his very own little showboat out into the middle of the lake and use it as a platform to make himself look very out there and switched on! This was virtue signalling at its very best leaving Piers Morgan no alternative then to storm off the set probably before he punched the smug little weather man from Lands End to John O Groats on his bloody weather map.

It could have been even worse though as I am sure once the little weather cock realised he was not going to get anywhere spouting his opinionated spiel to Mr Morgan he would have chucked in the race card and I am sure this would have left Piers with no alternative but to leave the show under a worse storm then he did with no way back into television, as it was Piers did the right thing probably egged on by the fabulous ITV team to just be a good boy and disappear for a while.

To write this chapter even I had to go back and Google why Piers resigned as I wanted my facts to be straight and to make sure I hadn't missed anything, such then was the insignificance of the spat that morning that even I had forgotten ☺

I look forward to Mr Morgan rearing his head somewhere on TV again or being brought back when the ITV ratings go way past the 'well actually no one is watching us anymore' so we better get Piers back quick scenario crops up.

As we have seen before with Mr Clarkson and now Mr Morgan you cannot be taken down by royalty or government ministers or indeed the public but upset a jumped up weatherman with as much charisma and panache as a breeze block and watch out Job Centre here you come, and what of this career marking too much to say about nothing weatherman? Where is he now?

After I am sure; hoping he would be slotted into Mr Morgan's shoes to take over as anchor man and after rocking the boat and causing all this trouble; Yep! He's still the bloody weatherman and why? Because any TV producer worth his salt would be crapping himself every time the weather cock fluffed his feathers and put someone else in an impossible position on live TV ☺

****

44

Wounded World of Woke!

A world where the victim is the one at fault; the perpetrator hides behind the good old ace card 'it wasn't me'

I didn't do it even when I did! If I keep telling myself and anyone who will listen long enough I didn't do it then I and them will believe it eventually.

The days of just putting your hands up and saying 'I was a Pratt' (no connection to my good and dear friend Darren☺) are now long gone; how dare anyone say I have done something; I am not to blame, it was my parents for not wiping my arse properly, it was my schooling because I never came first, I came third a few times but NEVER FIRST! It was my job; because I hate my job, I spend more time moaning about my job then I do working because they should all change for me and they won't, it was my friends because they never agreed with me and gave me support when I was being an absolute tooled up bell end, it was global warming because everyone blames that when they run out of things and people to blame.

We live then in a blame culture; instead of working hard, taking ownership of a problem some of us just pull down the blinds in our minds and say fuck it! It's definitely someone else's fault.

And why may you ask am I attempting to understand and bring this problem into the forefront of everyone's minds?

Well the story is long and to me very sharp at the moment; it doesn't have many players (fortunately) it concerns myself, my wonderful Assistance Dog 'Jerry' (He's the handsome chap on the back of the book) a Cockerpoo and a deluded owner who, you; guessed it blames everyone else but herself.

The long awaited haircut day had dawned after going through the stages of looking like Noel Edmunds then Grizzly Adams (thanks Nasher) I had booked the long overdue haircut, setting myself up for success I took Jerry for a quick toilet break before taking him with me to the barbers, where upon the poor little lad was attacked by a white exorcet missile Cockapoo.

45

Poor Jerry was bitten very badly, blood was pouring out of a wound on his right side, after quickly giving the very apologetic lady my telephone number and all thoughts of a long awaited haircut now gone into the stratosphere I bundled poor Jerry into the car and headed for the vets.

On arrival he was rushed into emergency surgery and after hours of nail biting time he came out of the anaesthesia and was eventually allowed home on painkillers and antibiotics.

Now to be fair to the other owner she did pay the vets bill, and made all the right noises being very apologetic and owning up to blame, things then were put on the back burner whilst Jerry recovered.

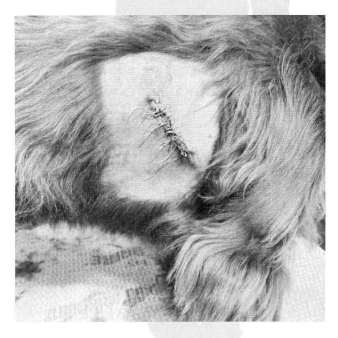

Three skin layers and 36 stitches later.

Now you will be reading this and thinking poor little lad, I bet that hurt and nice stitching job ☺ and this should be the end right?

As I explained before Jerry is my Assistance Dog and the laws on assistance dogs are slightly different, all attacks on assistance dogs need to be reported to the police so with advice from the charity I duly reported that my fully trained, passed the yearly public access test 5 years running, wouldn't hurt a fly, special lad had been attacked.

The police were absolutely fantastic, they kept me informed of their enquiries every step of the way and the outcome being that the owner would be dealt with under the dangerous dogs act and would have a muzzling order placed on her dog.

All well and good you may think, she had already admitted her dog being at fault by texts and by paying the vets bill so we can just get this dealt with in the right way and then all get on with our lives and put the whole traumatic incident behind us couldn't we?

Enter the world of WOKE! Once she realised her; some would say out of control dangerous dog was going to have to wear a muzzle the world of the victim is the bad person stepped into her gear; all of a sudden we were the bad ones for reporting her dog, we ceased to be the victims we were the devils reincarnate, how dare we blame her or her dog, the black and white story that had really unfolded that day in her world ceased to exist, now poor Jerry had cut himself on a piece of glass obviously held in the mouth of her dog as the wound was a good 10 inches from the ground on Jerry's flank or maybe it was her dogs identity disc that had caused the injury but there was no way on this earth that her dogs teeth caused that amount of damage.

She is now going to appeal the case because I am wrong, Jerry is wrong, the vet's receptionist is wrong, the veterinary nurses are wrong, the vet herself is wrong, the dog warden is wrong, the police are wrong in fact everybody involved with this case is wrong so where does that leave us? It leaves us

With a person that despite all the evidence to the contrary, her admission of guilt and paying the vets bill; because she is living in the land of bloody woke believes that her dog couldn't have possibly done that so now we have to go through it all again, through all the pain all the upset, now I don't mind telling you the reader; that I have a clinical diagnosis of PTSD (Post Traumatic Stress Disorder) I suffer horrendously with nightmares and lack of sleep, Jerry helps me through this and without him I would have hung myself from a tree years ago, sometimes it is so bad I feel I cannot possibly go on but I look at my Jerry and the thought of him being without me and having to live life without me looking after him stops me from actually taking my 'last jump' from a tree with a rope around my neck; it sounds dramatic but I am sure if it ever did happen it would be a fairly peaceful affair and a great release for me instead of having to live a life of constant mental torture and pain.

Now those of you that know me, see me getting on with life being as cheerful as I possibly can, owning up when I have been an utter pain in the bollocks and generally sometimes being an absolute wanker; I do not need the world of woke to hide behind, I do not need excuses; I am what I am; some people actually 'like' me ☺ or so I am told.

So you poor deluded person, reality is just what it is; reality; there is no world of woke just the real world, so suck it up and get on with owning up to your flaws we all have them, the difference is I guess some of us embrace and live with them.

You, and you know who you are; can shove your woke world up your arse!

****

Odd People

It seems very hip and almost normal these days to be 'odd', not quite with it, 'space cadets' we called them in the Army, people who walk around in a daze, you see them in my local supermarket, the very 'twee' people, who wouldn't say boo to a goose, they fanny around shopping looking confused at everything and anything, they dither and flit backwards and forwards totally oblivious to all that's going on around them, they wear sensible shoes and sensible clothes normally with designer labels on and always with the collar folded upwards? Always pastel colours to go with their completely pastel look

I find these people 'odd' I wonder how they ever get through a day without having a breakdown, of course most of these people shop on line now so to see one in the habitat of the local supermarket or street is a real treat, these people fascinate me and without them being there writing would be a lot harder.

Also walking around the village in absolute masses are 'old people' where have they all come from? They seem to be everywhere, since they were told to stay indoors and protect themselves they seem to be all over the place, as a retired soldier I am at home more than most and I never see many old people around, but there they are now, standing on street corners walking along pavements in a seemingly aimless quest to get infected, why are they out and about now? What is it about the request to stay at home that they don't understand? Maybe the older generation think it's like the Second World War, the; they don't like it up them and 'we will show that virus' bull dog spirit mentality!

MAMIS, no not the old fashioned show from yesteryear we are not allowed to mention anymore; these mammies are the dreaded Middle Aged Men in Spandex brigade, these blokes bring a whole new meaning to 'meat and two veg' as they squeeze their very unattractive and overweight bodies into the smallest size of cycling suit they can and hop on their cycles; some costing serious cash and head into the countryside, disregarding lockdown and social distancing as they meet up with their cycling spandex clad buddies...

Hoooo Rahhhh and head out on their 60 mile round trip to where ever nobody knows, the only thing I do know is that when I come driving around a blind corner and they are riding 4 abreast its extremely dangerous, chatting away and fist pumping each other I'm guessing congratulating themselves on another 60 miles done holding up the traffic and generally being bloody annoying to everyone.

During this very unsure time when doing my shopping I like to get in and get out as fast as possible at the local supermarket, but like the best laid plans they can go wrong, you grab your trolley, wait in the queue, spray your trolley down with disinfectant, scrupulously scrub your hands for 20+ seconds and await the starters flag to drop and away you go through the hallowed doors and your off!

Straight behind another shopper who is spending ages perusing and wondering which cauliflower to pick up or whether that bag of carrots has got more in it than that one, by the time they have made their bloody mind up there are 20 people behind you and them trying to self distance, you ask 'would you mind awfully if I went in front?' and Mrs Twee looks at you like a death star annoyed that you wish to go in front or make her hurry up with her choice, politeness tried and failed I revert back to Paratrooper, it's like a default button, 'Just get out of the fucking way you silly woman' there see, you've made me get angry when I was really trying to be nice!

After getting passed Mrs Twee you race around because she's held you and everybody else up for so long everyone else has finished their shopping, you run around like something out of supermarket sweep being shouted at by Dale Winton to go faster and then you bump into Mr Twat who completely ignoring the signs on the floor is coming the wrong way down the aisle FFS you swerve around Mr Twat who tutts at you because you crossed the 2 metre bubble he thinks he's got around him and you contemplate reminding him politely he's going the wrong way and then think to yourself, I remember being polite doesn't work so you shout at him your going the wrong way you TWAT he goes into complete meltdown because working in London all week he has never had to do the shopping before; his wife sent him out to get him from under her feet, he isn't good in supermarkets or on pavements, in fact he isn't good anywhere outside of London, in the Metropolis he is a whizz kid, one of the faithful, an absolute dynamo, in a supermarket he is just Mr Twat!

So around you go like some whirling dervish and then you come to the aisle that does all the shampoo and shower gel; now as 'proper' blokes know anything outside of Lynx is a conundrum, we shave, we shower, we run our fingers through are hair instead of a comb, we brush our teeth, anything other than that we are on shaky ground and now we have ground to a halt!

Why? We were doing so well, then we came to the shampoo aisle, the dreaded Mrs Twee has beaten you there by ignoring the signs on the floor, she is now deciding on hair colour, what shade to go next, shall I buy some conditioner, let me just check what it smells like, she spots me and looks down her very twee nose like a school teacher about to scold a pupil, it doesn't work with me I give her the 'one word from you and you are going to get both barrels you stuck up tart' look and whizz past on my way to freedom, I throw my small amount of shopping on the conveyor and pay my money and head for the door before I murder some F@@K.

I have a dog, he is a fully trained and qualified Assistance Dog his name is Jerry and he is bloody brilliant, a working cocker spaniel with more brains, compassion, love, intelligence and guts then most people I know, now as a qualified Assistance Dog by law I don't have to pick up his doggy waste but I do because it's the right and proper thing to do; I pick it up put it in a bag then I put it in a bin, then there are the others.

The ones who think it is OK to leave the dogs waste where it is, steaming in the middle of the path, because they are too posh to pick up or are just an absolute Chav!

There are ones who do pick it up, tie a nice knot in the bag and then throw it in the hedge or on the floor and then there are the 'special ones' these are

51

the morons who can throw their bag of doggy dos into the trees where it hangs proudly for all to see, like a trophy; a sign, yes a sign; a sign that some ignorant, selfish, filthy, moronic human being has been this way, I wonder what goes through these people's minds? You never see them do it, you never actually catch them in the act, it must take amazing skill to get that bag of your dogs shit into that tree like that, well done you; (more fist pumping) a very difficult and laudable thing to achieve, if I had my way and I caught you doing it Mrs Posh or Mr Chav I would make you climb that tree and get it down, so please Mrs Posh or Mr Chav; try and think about aiming it at a bin, you never know you may actually get it in first time and get the sense of achievement you obviously crave.

Some neighbours the other day were having a birthday party for little Johnny who is going to be 7, now this is lovely; even in lockdown they are going to have a little party for the lad, it warms the cockles of your heart doesn't it?

Until you find out that Johnny's little party consisted of a full blown BBQ with all Johnny's mates, all Johnny's mates parents all standing next to each other laughing, drinking, joking and spreading corona virus. Happy Birthday little Johnny let's hope you, your mates and all the parents; live to see your 8th birthday little man. ☺

Maybe these people were 'odd' anyway before corona virus came along and things have just been made worse or highlighted more, maybe these people are safely locked away somewhere and only allowed out during times of absolute emergency, perhaps they are just a little eccentric and the good old British eccentricity is fighting its way to the top, maybe it's the British stiff upper lip, laughing in the face of adversity.

Well when you take the chance of lying alone in a hospital Intensive Therapy Unit letting a ventilator breathe for you trying to fight off corona virus with a stiff upper lip, call me mad but I think THAT is very ODD

****

Justice for Jerry

So the day dawns when my little lad finally gets justice; after suffering an horrendous attack from another dog and despite still being terribly physically scarred Jerry will today learn the outcome of the enquires made by the police.

Nothing will take away the fact that he has not been able to wear his Assistance Dog jacket for over a month or the obvious slight fear and wariness of other dogs that creeps over him every time he goes out for a walk.

People that know Jerry will tell you that this is not the Jerry way, the happy, manic tail wagging, always up for a fuss and cuddle Jerry has lost some of his sparkle, some of his confidence and happiness died that day and despite always having the visible reminder of a scar I believe the real damage has been done deep within, despite nurturing him around and making him feel confident sometimes the fear in his eyes is very noticeable and this makes me very sad and the feeling of guilt will live with me forever, the guilt I have for not protecting him from the attack and not foreseeing the unforeseeable.

The local gendarmes have visited chez Mark and Jerry today for the final instalment of this very unhappy episode.

As a solution the offending dog owner has been 'invited' to sign a Community resolution Order which apparently she did with all the grace of having something nasty attached to the bottom of her shoe, this means she has to keep her dog under control at all times and on a lead, also the offending pooch will have to wear a muzzle when out in public; all this under these 'resolutions' come under the Dangerous Dogs Act; the vicious little sod will only have to wear muzzle for two years though after which presumably he will be free to bite some other poor dog, but in the meantime at least Jerry will be safe out walking, the woman thinks that her proven out of control dog has had an 'unjust' punishment levelled on it; so I am assuming that due to her logic she thinks that her vicious little thug biting Jerry was 'just' so it is 'just' that poor Jerry has to walk around with a scar, a slight fear of other dogs, perhaps she feels that Jerry should be the one on the lead and muzzled to make it easier for her little darling to have another go at the poor lad.

Obviously this is a very emotional subject but as far as I and the gendarmes are concerned this matter is now closed and the woman and the dog both got what they deserved; perhaps this will act as a warning to other dog owners who think it is OK to let their dogs run riot and out of control, but despite being in a reasonable mood today ☺ I very much feel like I am pissing in the wind ☺

A brave lad!

The Small Print

We live in a world of small print, it is everywhere from magazines to the television advertisements, so what is the purpose of this obvious necessity and must have in today's life?

As far as I can make out the purpose of small print is to protect the advertiser from being sued for spouting absolute bollocks!

Let us take into account certain well known advertisements, the one that uses a certain Irish charmless berk to have us believe that sitting with your feet on a plate on the floor and electrocuting them turns him from a couch potato into an instantaneous gazelle able to go for a long walk with his TV wife again; like a little lap dog in comfortable shoes and slacks all very twee and all very believable until you read the 'small print' which reliably informs you that it 'may not work for everybody' and 'you should seek your doctors permission' before you start using this miracle appliance, chances are you haven't read the small print, cannot get a doctor's appointment for love nor money, so thought fuck it I'm going to buy it anyway, it must be alright as its being advertised by a TV icon with his lovely twee wife playing a cameo role, they smile and comfortably chat and walk their way through the entire advertisement and give a little cheeky grin as if it will turn the aforementioned Irish berk; if she was very lucky into a raging sexual monster in the bedroom, because surely if it can turn him into the Country File version of Usain Bolt then with a little adaption and posturing it might have the same effect on other parts; wont it? Hopefully!

Forgive my obvious confusion but when did an innocent little chocolate coloured sweets become drugs? The day they made the TV advertisement showing kids swallowing what seems to be a well known sweet and being transported into a world of hallucinogenic mayhem.

This particular advertisement would have you believe that once you give your little darlings this particular once innocent delight, squirrel's start talking to you; you get highly coloured tree houses with everything the little loves ever wanted at the click of fingers within; the parents look like brightly coloured stupidly grinning clowns, you can eat the grass and the tree leaves, instantly the spaced out happy little ones have everything.

Now this worries me for the legal well being of this particular sweet maker, I maybe wrong but I think there may have been a breach of copyright laws somewhere, because back in the early nineties the last time my mate took a brightly coloured tablet and saw this amount of colour and hallucinogenic shenanigans was when he bought an acid tab off his dealer!

So I know I am old and probably well out of touch; but either you can buy the wrong kind of acid tablets for your kids from your local newsagent's sweet counter or this particular advertisement is just another example of absolute bollocks.

Whilst on the subject of small print and advertisements and finding myself in full flow; I feel; after a lot of piss taking from the general public and friends alike, that I have to point out and completely deny any involvement with a certain advertisement concerning two policemen eating jelly sweets in a patrol car parked at the side of the road! For the record this was not me or a certain other person who shall remain anonymous, isn't that right Nasher ☺

But my opinion for what it is worth (around 4 pence apparently☺) is that this particular advertisement all joking aside completely and utterly demeans the police force in this country, is it any wonder then that some of the public using all their 'common sense' actually believe this is real life! The same as some people believe that all American cops sit in their cars eating doughnuts and shooting defenceless law abiding people or arresting people for doing um 'nothing wrong' this makes the arresting officers the ones in the wrong, it makes the thieving, mugging, kidnapping, drug dealing, wife beating scum bags the victims and the people who are trying to protect the rest of us the bad ones, the world then in the words of a well know ex-television presenter 'has gone nuts' yes indeed everything we all knew and understood has been turned on its arse by a minority bunch of, tree hugging, left wing, some say intelligent, common sense lacking idiots, but that's just my opinion, isn't it ☺

What is a Hero?

In days gone by heroes won medals; they were legends, they charged machine gun emplacements with bayonets fixed and single handed saved a few good men to fight another day, sometimes they even got a medal, but mostly not.

Then there were the other heroes, the spitfire pilots high in the blue skies over Britain in 1940 fighting off the scourge of the Luftwaffe a much more superior enemy with more planes and pilots, leaving vapour trails in the sky as they circled, dived and fought their way in and out of battle, and then returning home, shot up and tally hoed in time for bacon and eggs before they went back up and did it all again.

Then there are the heroes who run into burning buildings to rescue mothers and babies, the heroes that ran towards the twin towers in New York when they knew they were collapsing around them, the heroes that risk their lives every day to fight fires or cut people from crashed cars.

Other heroes include the modern day service personnel who went to fight to keep the country safe, leaving behind their families, friends and loved ones, going out from behind the walls day after day, putting themselves in the firing line to be shot at and bombed never knowing if they would see jolly old England again, receiving no medals but being left with horrific injuries and PTSD! coming home to a country with no care, no treatment and certainly no medals, they were just doing their job the public and Government says and that is why we never complain or like to be called heroes.

But now we have a different kind of hero, ones that are doing their job, the doctors, the nurses, the bin men, the pharmacist, the road sweepers, the postman, the supermarket workers, all in the new 'front line' and all very much appreciated and thought of, but heroes?

I beg to differ; calling everyone a hero dilutes and cheapens heroes of past, it makes a mockery of the heroic exploits that make this country **GREAT.**

Will we still be talking about the so called hero postman in 20/30/40 year's time? I doubt it, but we will still be talking about the brave, heroic spitfire pilot rolling, ducking and diving and leaving vapour trails in the blue skies of this wonderful country defending our spirit and way of life.

Especially this year 2020 celebrating the 75th Anniversary of VE Day

As David Bowie once said; we can be heroes, just for one day!

****

"A hero is someone who has given his or her life to something bigger than oneself."

Joseph Campbell

Cummings and Goings

Much has been and continues to be said about Dominic Cummings; the man that supposedly broke all the rules and travelled to Durham for what seems like a 'jolly nice week' on his parent's farm (how lovely) and then just to make sure he caused as much confusion and division as possible; he took his wife and kids out for a lovely picnic to Barnard Castle!

Picture the scene sitting on the bank of the river having an absolutely wonderful time soaking up the sun lounging by a babbling river watching the twigs float by, feeding the ducks and spending quality time with his family.

In any other time this scenario would have been idyllic, a peaceful and probably well earned break from the stress, torment and tribulations of a Government Minister in the middle of a worldwide pandemic.

Enter stage left Cummings; obviously either an absolute buffoon or a complete and utter undeniable liar, making the ultimate cock up and committing the ultimate sin that is; **'getting caught'**

The British public god bless them are not as stupid and unlearned as you would have liked to have thought; probably down to a college/university education system given to all over the last 20/30 years or so.

Being well educated comes with the ability to question, the ability to have a voice and the intelligence to know when somebody is spinning you an absolute 'bounder'

So what did Cummings do when he got caught in the act of breaking his very own guidelines? Instead of holding his hands up and saying 'I've been an absolute Boris' (or words to that effect) he spun out in front of the worlds press some fantastical story and plot that even a half baked Hollywood film producer would have thrown back at him with a raised eyebrow and uttering those immortal words 'are you fucking sure'?

What we are all by now absolutely sure of (Mr) Cummings is that you **do not** travel all the way to Durham with a sick child, you seek out medical help from the nearest facility and you **do not** get in your car and drive to a beauty spot to test your eyesight (Lucky you had a picnic in the boot though) ☺ and then drive back just to make sure, that's just like saying I drove home drunk just to test how drunk I was.

Are we really expected to believe a so called 'intelligent' Government Minister drove his car to test his eyesight, is this how our schools, colleges and universities are teaching nowadays? It makes my comprehensive education seem very real, right and spot on doesn't it!

But all this is conjecture and unsubstantiated waffle, either Cummings is too intelligent for us to understand, to thick to know the difference between right and wrong, to arrogant to follow his own advice or just plain and simple a really bad liar; the British people will make their own mind up.

We are not all fools as you have learnt to your cost, although as we see with some of the children today we have grown another consequence; in this our wonderful country, children who lie and steal with no fear of punishment, children who lose at the egg and spoon race at school but receive a 'participation' medal so their feelings are not hurt, no wonder then that Cummings can blatantly lie and keep his job, blatantly lie and arrogantly expect the British people to believe it, all this shows our children whatever you do wrong there is **NO** consequence; how long will it be before you hear those immortal words in front of a custody sergeant at a police station near you 'well Cummings did it and got away with it'

And here we are again; today the liar that is Cummings has reared his ugly head despite being labelled a proven teller of untruths to give some juicy evidence (lies) to a select committee and everyone is waiting to see what the nasty little grassing shit spews out next! Poor Boris; you defended a wrongun!

****

Common Sense

I have looked everywhere; scoured the shops; lifted every stone; rooted every cupboard; turned the country upside down; been frustrated and blanked at every turn.

So; what have I been looking for you may well ask; money, toilet rolls, hand gel, face masks, nope the one thing that is harder to find then a Government Minister with a straight answer; welcome to my hunt for the elusive Common Sense!

Common Sense is the one thing that keeps people safe; it makes people think before acting, so the young lads who tombstone off a 40 foot bridge into 12 inches of water and wonder why they end up paralysed from the neck down take note! Or the cyclist that rides down the inside of a Lorry's blind spot when it is negotiating a left turn and wonder why they get crushed maybe they should think about 'common sense'

The lack of common sense has led to another phenomenon; the capacity to blame anything and anybody else but yourself for being an absolute twat; so the moron on the bridge will blame the bridge builder, the lack of warning signs, the depth of the water due to climate change (double blame there ☺) the authorities for not being there and holding his hand and advising him he may hurt himself and not having the proper 'procedures' in place in case some 'spanner' despite all that warning wanted to jump in anyway.

But the blame moves on in a mysterious way! If the authorities put up fencing, barbed wire, anti climb poles and paint on the bridge to stop the 'tool' from jumping, he will claim his view has been spoilt, the safety barriers are infringing on his human rights to be an absolute 'fooktard' his fun has been spoilt, he is angry and upset that someone should care that he hurts himself, it's his body and he can be a fucking moronic spanner wielding tool if he wants.

The cyclist who failed to read the Highway Code or was home on the X Box the day they did the cycling proficiency test at school and therefore failed to

Learn about the bit that says 'you must not undertake on the left unless a vehicle is turning right'

Ergo; the poor lorry driver has failed to see the cyclist in his obvious blind spot moving up his left hand side and everyone is then surprised when the cyclist gets maimed or killed when the lorry turns left, but instead of the cyclist being at fault for not overtaking on the right like any normal person with common sense; people start to blame everybody and everything else.

The lorry driver for not expecting a cyclist to put themselves in danger and undertake; the haulage company for failing to put a sign on the rear of the lorry big enough for a complete knob to read assuming the idiot could read anyway (take that how you want) or the authorities not enforcing any of these things, maybe if the rule of the road was made clear about undertaking and a few enforcements carried out people wouldn't put themselves in danger, but then we would be accused of running the country like a police nanny state.

It seems common sense nowadays is about as rare as finding gold at the bottom of your garden water butt; but in the true fashion of my scribbling I will give you all some common sense for free; you see I have never lost it and I have oodles of it to share; **DO NOT** jump from a bridge into shallow water (my granddad taught me that one) and god forbid if you ever want to get on a bicycle; **DO NOT** undertake a lorry turning left (common sense and survival taught me that one ☺)

Please look out for my new forthcoming book entitled:

COMMON SENSE - The Dark Art

I do fear though that it may take me quite a long time to write as some of you are going to have to start from scratch; and if you do get the urge to drive your car 30 miles when your eyesight is bad; maybe common sense says 'take the bus' ☺

****

PTSD The Forward

Nightmares; anxiety, flashbacks, just some of the symptoms of PTSD also know as Post Traumatic Stress Disorder; but in reality in a family environment these equate to some very real symptoms of anger, emotional outbursts, crying, irritability, fear of crowded places, anxiety brought on by the f - - king numbskull tailgating the rear of your car, (which seems to becoming a national past time), sitting with your back to the wall in pubs and restaurants everywhere you go; this list then is endless and not nearly complete here; if any of this sounds familiar to you; welcome to a very exclusive club.

The real consequence to suffering with PTSD is we react to danger differently now; so although angry outbursts are frowned upon nowadays and seen as 'un-cool' in a world of 'sensitive' and newly 'awoke' men; we are monsters; is it any wonder that some of us maybe a bit broken, a bit insensitive to death, pain, hurt and your feelings?

Some of us have come home de-sensitised, oblivious to your 'dramas' things that you think are life and death, to some of us seem trivial this does not mean we don't care or value your feelings we just find it hard to adjust to your way of life.

To try and help people to understand us a bit better I have asked a good friend of mine, a combat brother who I served with for many years to tell one of his stories, I say 'just one' because he has many, many stories of horror, many stories of adventure, many stories of comradeship and some funny stories to go with them, when in some people's eyes he has returned a monster, not the happy, very funny bloke that went away to fight for his country and his fellow soldiers but came home the product of an evil; horrible war that left us all with a bad taste in our mouths.

Read his story without judgement and with an open mind, take on board the description of his experiences and have some understanding as to why this and many other stories still give him nightmares and flashbacks to this day.

This is a real story written in a real moment in time with real facts as it happened, a very real battle to save the life of a British Diplomat during an assassination attempt at the Ministry of Justice in Kabul Afghanistan.

PTSD The Story

Afghanistan (Kabul).

Can't remember what the date was, or what day it even was they always seemed to merge into one, until it was time to come home of course.

On this day we were on QRF (Quick Reaction Force) at the British Embassy Kabul.

We had had our team brief from Vic Moon. It consisted of two times two man teams.

Team one Nasher & Dan and Team two James & Gluepot, same shitty atmosphere (Literally) hot and sticky.

We knew what teams were out on the ground, and what AOO (Area of Operations) we were expected to go to give support if required.

It started, with this almighty fucking bang followed by the putt putt of automatic fire off in the distance, we grabbed our kit and dived outside to get the Bobby Moore, to see Vic Moon bounding over to us to give us the good news.

The MOJ has been attacked with a British Diplomat and Interpreter and 2 CPO's (Close Protection Officers) at that location (Taff & Pete).

Basically, get our arses down there and give assistance to our guys, and get out soonest. Keep in communication at all times, we would get updates on the way from the TOC.

Another (QRF) crash out in Afghanistan. However, this is different, as our mates are in trouble, people we know personally. We fight our way through the Kabul traffic, which Dan & Gluepot do without exception. We are two blocks/streets away before we come to a complete stand still, James comes over the radio that we aren't going anywhere and we need to go foxtrot (Walking).

We leave the Vehicles with Dan & Gluepot and brief them to get to the MOJ (Ministry of Justice) ASAP. Now at this point, you should know James is a 6ft 7ins man fucking mountain and Nasher (Me) is 5ft 6in on a good day. I advise James to lead the way and tuck in behind his slip steam, at this point I'm doubling to each of his strides. We reach the outside gates of the MOJ, hot, sweaty and ready to face the uncertainty of what's behind those gates.

The first sight that greets us of this senseless devastation is 5 ANP (Afghan National police) mutilated bodies that we have no choice but to step over very carefully so as not to move the bodies, or get covered with blood and bits of flesh, we tried but not successful. Once through the gate it was like walking into a gun fest automatic fire and explosions from all 4 corners of the courtyard.

Taking cover behind the Armoured SUV that had been left by our muckers. By this stage we had been given updates that Taff was inside with the Diplomat & Interpreter, and Pete was outside with the vehicle. Vehicle found but no Pete. We could see that the vehicle had been struck by something on the windscreen but hadn't gone off.

So, above the noise we started shouting and looking for Pete, who we found right behind us in the corner the MOJ garage. Pete joined us at the SUV and briefed us on what had happened.

Pete informed us that the attack came from the main gate; He was sat at the driver's wheel when an explosion had happened at the front gate, he took cover in the foot well and saw a bloke with an RPG take aim at the SUV, fired the grenade launcher which hit the windscreen and ricocheted into the courtyard and exploding. He waited for the fire to suppress before he checked his 5 & 20's (Surrounding Area) before leaving the vehicle and taking cover in the MOJ garage. Now we are a force of 3 (Amigos) against a force only God would know at this moment in time.

We take up fire positions on the driver's side (LHD) and take in, the playing field to our front. We learn from Pete that Taff/Diplomat and Interpreter have made their way downstairs and taking refuge in a stationary cupboard after being left by the Afghan minister they were visiting.

We can see ANP police climbing up ladders to the windows of the MOJ buildings in front of us and being shot off the ladders. The ones that do get through are then blasted back out through the windows, taken out almost immediately with automatic fire and grenades.

Whilst waiting for permission to go in from British Embassy, a lone shot streaks across the front of all 3 of us from right to left and thuds into the rear wall of the MOJ, just missing the Afghan ANP commander. The next thing we know, these coppers have turned their AK47's on us and shouting and screaming. We lower our own AK's and I approach the commander shouting at each other that we didn't fire that shot and we are here to help them in this rescue mission.

All 3 of us then approached the ANP commander, and explain to him that if a shot had been fired by us, then our AK barrels would be warm to touch, he understood what we were saying and checked each of our AK barrels, all the time a gun battle was raging in the MOJ building to our front. Then another shot rang out just above our heads hitting the same wall. We all looked to our right, to see this very young ANP soldier having trouble with his AK and having ND's (Negligent Discharge) each time he cocked the rifle (he had not removed the magazine). The Afghan commander pushed us aside and went over a started beating the young lad, screaming obscenities about him and his family donkey/goat?

We took up our fire positions once again and regained communications with Taff, now Taff couldn't chat over the radio, as he had a heavily armed terrorist just outside the stationary door cupboard. We found this out by a serious of questions with two for yes and one for no clicks on the radio.

The Afghan commander had now received his ANP (SF) reinforcements, these guys were so poorly equipped but were brave as hell, they were briefed by the Afghan commander and went straight in the double doors bunched together, within a 30-45 seconds, another loud explosion with automatic fire was heard and felt by us outside, the remaining SF came running out in clip, the Afghan commander started to beat them and throw them back into the building. (unbelievable ☺).

The next thing that stopped us in our tracks was the Afghan Ambulance Service, whilst the commander was still beating his men and trying to get them back inside the building, these 2 guys came running through the main gate at each end of the stretcher, and straight into the building.

Within 3-4 minutes s they emerged somewhat grey in colour with 2 Afghan National Policeman on one stretcher, as they run out one of the policeman's heads kept separating in half with each bounce of the stretcher.

(Thank f - - k breakfast had been eaten many hours earlier).

We could see this shit wasn't going anywhere, and we knew it was our turn to go in and get our mucker and clients. However, the gun fire and internal explosions had decreased since the ambulance staff had come out. We had now been given the green light by the Embassy to go in, but to keep communications open.

We informed the Afghan commander we were going in and we hope to bring out 3 Males. We formed up outside in single file and made our way slowly into the building, the smell and heat hits you first of all cordite, burnt flesh, trying to keep your feet and balance on the tiled floor with the amount of blood that has been spilled, gives Dancing on Ice a new meaning.

Now, it's at this point I have forgot to mention that in our haste to get our guys out, we formed up with James in front (6ft 7in) 2nd Pete (6ft 3in) 3rd Me (5ft 6in on a good day). You can imagine I can't see diddly squat and looks like I'm doing an Irish jig, trying to see around and above my two colleagues in front of me. I stop the guys and mention this to them and under stifled laughter (nerves) we swap positions, Me, Pete, James (Makes sense).

We make our way to the top the stairs, having cleared the corridors right and left bodies everywhere not moving. Running commentary, Taff at the top of the stairs, (double click) Taff moving down the stairs, (double click) as we get to the midsection of the stair case, we can see the ground floor, and a lone door with a staircase running up the right hand side as you look at it, with a pair of dirty lifeless feet with one flip-flop attached.

I explain to Taff where we are in the building and that we have a lone door in front of us (double click). Now, we know that Taff has only his side arm for defence as no longs are allowed into the MOJ (bet that changes, after this) the area is really creepy quiet, not a sound apart from the odd settling noise of the building that's just been beaten to f - - k. No shouting, no screaming.

So, I ask Taff, to make his way to door of his hiding place (double click), hoping that by any luck we have the right door first time round. I ask Taff to open his door very slowly and produce his side arm for view (double click). The door opens slowly, and a pistol appears, we have them. I tell Taff to prepare to make a run for it up the stairs directly In front of his door. Stand by Stand by (Yes, I said it twice) Go Go Go, the door burst open with Taff half covering his client and half leading the charge up the stairs dragging his Diplomat with Interpreter attached.

At this point James is in front bounding up the stairs 3-4 at a time with Taff and party close behind with Pete and me bringing up the rear. As we break into the light of the day, I see James rifle butt the Afghan commander who has decided to grab our Interpreter/Diplomat (WTF) was he thinking. We were like a forward scrum pushing our way forward to the main gate, knocking over anybody who tried to get in our way. I was also screaming to James the vehicles were now outside the main gate waiting for ex filtration a Black & Silver SUV with Dan & Gluepot. True to their word the two vehicles were there.

Doors opened and slammed shouts of commands go go go, but we sat there. I looked across to Dan, 'who the fuck are you'? And where is Dan?

'I'm sorry this is not your vehicle' no Shit Sherlock". I think they are your vehicles said the Afghan driver pointing 50-75 meters to our front same colour, same make, would you Adam and Eve it FFS ☺

Doors opened; loads more shouting and another sprint to the other two vehicles driven by Dan & Gluepot, clients loaded doors closed **GO GO GO**. Within seconds we were pissing ourselves laughing, a hostage rescue without a shot fired. Taff asking for permission to have a fag in the Embassy vehicle, fuck it we all had one, even those that didn't smoke.

We made it back to the British Embassy without further incident, to a full debrief, and me getting my knuckles rapped for not realising my language over the radio, was somewhat not procedure, but hey we made it.

****

PTSD The Afterword by Nasher

I have been asked to write this; one of many incidents that has happened throughout the 15 years on the circuit.

I suffer from PTSD, and it's not always the same night terrors, the story has a strange way of changing itself in your brain, with different outcomes of the nightmare for the better sometimes.

I can't say whether writing this story has helped, although it did bring some emotions to the surface. I'm lucky that I have someone to talk to (Bruvafromanothermother) when I can't get hold of the trick cyclist. Which I have to admit is a struggle to get hold of some time, as I know they are busy.

I believe more should be done for our veteran's male/female and believe that if a government sends you to any war/conflict, they should be there to help on your return and at any cost.

I know this will probably fall on deaf ears, PTSD is a real injury/sickness that not only covers all of our Armed Forces, it also covers: Police, Fire, Ambulance and hospital services.

Last note to all whatever and wherever you may be stay safe and come home soon.

****

A man who is good enough to shed his blood for his country is good enough to be given a square deal afterwards. More than that no man is entitled to, and less than that no man shall have.

(Theodore Roosevelt)

Does owning a Cockapoo make you Posh?

Now I consider myself extremely lucky! I have had the good fortune to live in a really nice village for 25 years; nice people, nice pubs, great shops, loads of country walks on my doorstep, all the houses have parking spaces and wonderful tree lined streets.

But now we have a massive influx of people buying new houses in the village taking up our green spaces and walks with urbanisation, land sold on by farmers who have always wondered what to do with that field they have laid fallow all those years; it seems the house building companies can build on anything and anywhere with no thought for the impact it will have on our schools, the environment and our services.

Now before you all start shouting NIMBY; I fully understand that there are people who would love to live in my nice oasis of a village and share my adoration for all things country but this is exactly what it is 'the country' the clue is in the title, we do not have cinemas, swimming pools, adventure parks and shopping centres; some people are strange though they move from a town to the country but want to turn the country into a town; along with this 'townie' phenomenon comes all the must have country trappings, a Volvo XC90, a train season ticket, drug dealers, violence, crime and the worst thing of all the 'put on' common 'plum posh' accent.

And then we have the cherry on top of the cake the final trinket of countryside accruement the Cockapoo! Gone are the days of the Staffie squeezed into a studded leather harness, a stolen Ford Sierra and barricades on every street corner; in our village we are so posh we build hedgehog houses out of bricks, not throw them at police ☺

No self respecting newbie then would dare to be seen out and about without a Costa Coffee cup, a set of Volvo XC90 keys, green knee length wellie's and a Cockapoo!

But does buying into the lifestyle make you that person? Keeping up with the 'joneses' or whatever double barrelled name you have nowadays can be an expensive business; your average rescue dog from a reputable dog rescue centre charity will probably cost you around £200 where as your average Cockapoo in the village should you be able to find any to buy will cost you around £3750 and with the 'invent' of lockdown and Covid the Cockapoo has become almost as sought after as a negative Covid test and expensive as the XC90 you are driving around in because after all you live in the country now don't you and you are bound to need a fuel guzzling tractor to get you out of tricky situations like … well like … well you know as you bought one ☺

So back to the title and original question which sparked all this scratching on paper with a pen 'does owning a Cockapoo make you posh?'

I'm finding it extremely hard to answer that question with any certainty of being right but I remember my old headmaster saying to me once during yet another visit to his office for words of 'advice' **'you cannot buy class'** and **'Lanchbery if you cannot be bright always have shiny shoes'**?

That from a headmaster who used to cane me for asking too many questions, so somewhere in these scribblings; my sore caned backside and my headmaster's wisdom lays the truth☺.

****

Winner Winner Chicken Dinner

Outside it is cold; raining and miserable, life is hard going, people are angry with each other the world over, corona virus, face masks, money is short, jobs are at risk, confusion and fear reign, inconsistency, uncertainty running rife, pandemics, lockdowns, hatred, demonstrations, scammers, stabbers, shooters, government mis-information, thuggery, muggery, theft; we have had it all in the last six months, is there anything that can change this landslide of misery? Can anything make things seem just a little better even for just a little while?

Winning the lottery, a pay rise at work, constant sunshine, a nice holiday, a new car, a new home or a new partner all these things would be nice but would they make things seem better, would they put a smile on your face?

No; the one thing that can always make you smile after a hard day at work, a hard day just trying to survive in a hostile world is when you open the door and smell that elusive smell of all smells, the fantastic smell of a winner winner roast chicken dinner.

So where did the phrase winner winner chicken dinner originate from?

Winner winner chicken dinner is a phrase that originated from the gambling casinos of Las Vegas who had a three piece chicken dinner which consisted of a piece of chicken a potato and a vegetable on their menus for the princely sum of $1.79, a standard bet in the casino back then was $2 hence when you won a bet you had enough for a chicken dinner! And the call used to go out around the casino winner winner chicken dinner.

There is nothing like the smell and taste of chicken skin browning in the oven; maybe with a coating of Herb's de Provence to add that French BBQ flavour and smell, the sizzling of homemade roast potatoes roasting in the pan going nice and crispy on the outside and warm and fluffy on the inside.

A warm fire when it is raining and cold outside, a nice cold beer or glass of wine as an aperitif whilst you take in all the fantastic smells wafting around the house, this is the stuff of the chicken dinner; each individual aroma separating in the nostrils and teasing the senses, no wonder then even the most basic and easy of meals to construct makes everyone feel warm and cosy; at home and a 'winner'

So when life seems a bit crap and everything seems a real hard grind do not despair, put a chicken in the oven gas mark 6 for around an hour and a half pour yourself a cold beer or a glass of wine, kick back and relax and enjoy being a 'winner' ☺

Great Britain – Just Love it!

Demonstrations on the streets of Great Britain were always going to come to violence.

It did so because, ultimately, that's what a massive proportion of those who attended the marches wanted.

Not content with graffitiing on the Cenotaph, urinating on Churchill's statue, shouting 'scum' at the people who were stood around guarding the other statues on Whitehall, spreading COVID-19, or demanding spineless coppers kneel before them like Superman knelt before General Zod, they were seeking the prize of direct confrontation. So allow me to re-iterate a few truths here that the media have carefully ignored.

Firstly, racism is a **TWO-WAY** phenomenon in this country. People of every ethnic background have suffered and still suffer it. A few years ago, I was called a 'white c - - t by a young Asian guy I had challenged in a 'nice' town over his dangerous and reckless driving. I am sure many others could give you similar stories.

The overwhelming majority of white people are not racist. But neither are we going to apologise or possess some sort of idiotic guilt complex because of our identity, our history or this country.

As the excellent MP Kemi Badenoch (a Londoner of Nigerian parentage) said the other day: 'Britain is one of the best countries in the world to be a black person.' She's right! If the UK was some sort of dysfunctional, contemporary version of Sparta, Mississippi awash with institutional racists, do we honestly believe thousands and thousands of people from across the world would be so keen to come and live here every year?! By the same measure, do we think outstanding public figures such as Kemi Badenoch, Rishi Sunak or Priti Patel would have had the same chance of achieving so much had their parents not decided to emigrate to Britain?

My own late great uncle Rick came to the UK from Jamaica after fighting in the RAF in WW2, married into the family, and eventually ended up being one of the top bods at the Inland Revenue in Manchester. That opportunity would not have been possible had he stayed in Jamaica.

Ethnic minorities developed in the UK because their forefathers come to this country for a better life and greater opportunities. The vast majority recognise that fact and are appreciative of it.

But a hardcore minority (usually 2nd or 3rd British-born generations of the political Left) have a chip on their shoulder of Venus de Milo proportions. Put them together with armies of pasty-faced horrible white middle-class adolescents, schooled by Lefty teachers and then by Lefty professors into adopting an incomprehensible hatred of their country and everything it stands For, and you have the sort of toxic mixture you witnessed exploding on to the streets of central London.

Secondly, this has never been about black versus white. That's just a flag of convenience for a venal media class luxuriating in Left-wing agitprop. This is about chaos versus order; civilised values versus a violent mob; democracy versus pseudo-communistic authoritarianism and the rule of the cult; extremism versus moderation. We're living in an age when, with the notable exception of current government circles, so many have to tolerate an oppressive political environment nurtured by the chatterati.

One where even the slightest deviation from consensus opinion could result in career-ending consequences and the destruction of their livelihoods. Where police misconduct has blatantly occurred - whether in this country or elsewhere - you allow due judicial process to deal with the transgressor.

You don't jump on the bandwagon of imagined or grossly exaggerated grievance, and then use that to foment mob rule and the silencing of any remotely dissenting opinion.

Finally, we've also seen over the past few weeks, hundreds of thousands of Hong Kong Chinese demonstrate their loyalty to Britain and to British values in the face of repression from a Beijing administration all too willing to rip up every international treaty in the book.
I then propose a solution: Let those entrepreneurial, patriotic, democracy-loving Hong Kongese and their families come and start new lives in a country they so obviously love.

In return, let's encourage the uncultivated battalions of professional jeremiad composers - white, black or of any other background - to go and try life under Chinese communism for a while, just to give them a flavour of what hardship really is like. Because as far as I'm concerned, I don't give a damn what skin colour you are.

This is about respect for the flag below and the country it represents. If you're incapable of performing that very basic requirement of citizenship, and are willing to trash and traduce the symbols of our country at the flick of an emotional switch, then get the hell out of here and go and live somewhere else.

****

By kind permission of 'Steve' the real voice of Britain today!

80

The Cycling Scourge

Tour De France; cycle racing on roads in the UK (allowed but unsafe?) the two wheeled wonders call it 'time trialling' I call it out and out racing! Racing against each other or racing against a clock it is still racing and in my and many others opinion the scourge of British roads.

We are not talking about the family cycling together down quiet country lanes on various size bikes with a lovely picnic to be had in a field or a nice lunch in a quiet country pub somewhere; this type of cycling is a wonderful pastime; a great family team building exercise, a great way to spend time together and increase that bond that is the family unit!

This is the stuff of Enid Blyton's Famous Five and the pastimes of English families since time began, the wicker baskets, the fresh crusty bread, potted meat and soda pop an absolute picture to behold, family cycling at its very best, cycling that should be encouraged, nurtured and protected at all costs.

And then we have the other type!

The spandex clad 'Tour De France' wannabe, money no object latest, lightest cycling machine, arrogant, ignorant, self centred, entitled, unaware road thieves, they pay NO road tax, NO insurance and probably have NO licence to drive anything on the road (Judged by the way they disregard the laws and Highway Code) they go through red lights, cut across roundabouts, do not bother to indicate which way they might turn (it spoils their slipstream apparently) they wear clothing which is about as visible as the very latest stealth bomber; expecting the motorist to see and avoid them at all costs at the peril of being sued by some insanely expensive lawyer who also loves wearing spandex strictly on a weekend basis on our congested, contested and over used roads.

They generally have no regard for other road users, in fact with their entitled attitude and arrogance they are bordering on the downright dangerous.

They flout just about every law going by 'time trialling; their way across our green and pleasant land (because we cannot call it racing☺)

These are a different breed of cyclist; they have found just about every loophole in the law and are abusing the said laws at every opportunity; please take some helpful advice as I like to end on a positive note, you my cycling friend are not in the Tour de France despite your ebay bought spandex slightly too small suit which depicts you are, you are not even in France, what you are is a pain in the arse (excuse the pun ☺) you rub grease into your arse cracks; pull on your ever so tight spandex and mount your £1000 plus machine and have the entitled arrogant belief that every other road user must get out of YOUR way or else, **SOME** of you are a menace and I am amazed some of you have not been prosecuted, perhaps if the points went onto your car driving licence and you had any chance of being caught you would **THINK** and be more careful, thoughtful and have less arrogance, you have no more right to be on the roads then any of us so please just have a bit of thought or as I am suspecting this maybe just be **WISHFUL THINKING** on my part ☺

The Cycling Scourge Part II

Here we go again! Since last writing way way back last year has the situation regarding these spandex clad pests got any better?

Well here we are now in February 2021 and the cycling menace has got much worse along with the in clandestine weather, yet another lockdown (Apologies for the use of the Americanism) and a pandemic that just refuses to go away.

Today the news is full of this country reaching the 100,000 deaths marker and yesterday we had 1631 deaths in the UK, so how do the spandex clad morons celebrate these mammoth milestones? They go out on their bloody bikes to spread even more covid 19 amongst the populace.

There they are allegedly working from home (bollocks) or self isolating (more bollocks) or unable to go into work because transport isn't safe enough (even more bollocks)

What they are doing is using this time like some cycling bloody holiday, riding around the countryside with no lights on their bikes, no hi visibility clothing and no bloody idea! I came across one last week in thick fog on a country lane wearing a grey spandex suit with no lights at all, as it was foggy my speed was minimal and I have good eyesight, around 5 yards away this moronic specimen appeared out of the fog and I just managed to swerve to avoid him, I politely lowered my window and tried to inform him that I only just saw him in time and that he wasn't very visible to traffic, I was politely told to fuck off and mind my own business!

So fuck off I did; wondering if one of the increasing amount of 'older' people driving around on that road to go to the 'essential' garden centre would have the eyesight or the reaction time of yours truly.

But still that wasn't my problem as people keep telling me 'you cannot teach stupid' and with this I am starting to agree, these arrogant people will not be told, they are living in the bubble spurred on by yet more Government clap trap that cycling should be encouraged and cycling is the way of the future, if cycling was the way of the future then why did we invent cars?

I understand people need to get out and about to exercise, but the question I also ask myself is did these people exercise when they were in their offices in London or elsewhere? Probably not, but all of a sudden they have become the exercise gurus of the land, the cycling crowd, the in vogue people, the ahead of the curve go to lads and lasses, the Government telling everyone to STAY AT HOME during a lockdown does not apply to them because Boris told them to get 'on their bikes' so any 'order' after that is null and void.

People will do what they want to do now and always find an excuse for anything; Cummings saw to that and things will not change now, this lockdown is a joke there are more people out there now then there would be on a normal pandemic free day, but if you are one of the spandex clad good cyclists then thank you for being responsible people and enjoy your ride, but if you are one of the irresponsible, arrogant, no lights, no proper clothing, road thieving morons thinking we as vehicle drivers owe you a space and are so entitled to be there then **you** fuck off and mind your own business, I will write what I like because as you exploit every day to your full advantage we live in a democracy.

Inconsistency

STAY AT HOME

EAT OUT TO HELP OUT

DON'T MAKE UNNECESSARY TRIPS

(THAT DOESN'T APPLY TO MY FRIEND DOMINIC CUMMINGS)

GO TO WORK

WORK FROM HOME

GO BACK TO WORK

BUY YOUR LUNCH FROM PRET

STOP GOING TO CAFES

WORK FROM HOME

WHAT TRACK AND TRACE SCHEME?

GOING TO THE PUB MEANS YOU LOVE ENGLAND

STOP GOING TO THE PUB

WEAR MASKS INDOORS

EXCEPT IN PUBS AND RESTAURANTS

BUT DON'T GO TO PUBS AND RESTAURANTS

NO GROUPS OF MORE THAN 6

UNLESS YOU'RE HUNTING GROUSE

GO TO SCHOOL WHERE YOU CAN MINGLE WITH 300+ OTHER STUDENTS

BUT IF YOU LEAVE THE GATES IN A GROUP OF 7 YOU'LL BE ARRESTED

WHY WON'T BRITONS LISTEN TO MY CLEAR ADVICE?

STAY INCONSISTENT   PRIORITISE THE ECONOMY ABOVE LIVES   SHIFT BLAME

I have tried to be as objective about the Government and inconsistency as I can, but since Dominic Cummings took his little trip nothing has been the same again, there is no doubt he should have been sacked or at the very least reprimanded by Boris but he managed to swerve that, the Government have failed to admit anything probably through fear of being sued or looking totally inept and facing the wrath of the British press and media.

But; would it not have been better to throw yourself to the mercy of the British public and moved on with integrity and purpose, there are some people who are using this absolute chaos to their advantage and there are some people without doubt dying.

Either way I am sure it is not unsalvageable but the daily drivel that is trawled in front of us is wearing a bit thin, we need purpose and drive to have any hope of getting out of this pandemic with our heads held high, throwing money at the situation is counting on peoples greed to keep them quiet and we have already seen the greed and dishonesty of some people who will even steal by claiming Government grants to which they have scammed their way into.

We also saw this type of behaviour after the Grenfell disaster, people claiming money and assistance even though they were not even there, is it any wonder then that SOME of these people feed from the bottom? The lowest of the low whom will take full advantage of any 'disaster' and divert funds away from the people who really need and deserve it.

You do get a feeling though that poor old Boris is being pulled this way and that listening to some very dubious people, if he is listening to someone who likes to test his eyesight by driving to a beauty spot or thinks it's ok to spin a yarn in front of the world's media is it any wonder that inconsistency probably started right there, just as the right honourable gentlemen ☺ was inconsistent with his little 'story' about his road trip he may be feeding poor Boris even more inconsistent claptrap.

If inconsistency was ever going to get us out of a pandemic this Government would be at the top of the tree now instead of grubbing around underneath it searching for the next snazzy ditty to amaze the populace.

****

86

Afterword

I have thought long and hard about writing about such emotive subjects and really just started it as a way of getting myself through PTSD and COVID 19, it was a way of charting my progress, it helped me a great deal to see in a clear and precise way what was going on in the world and it some small way start to put things in perspective.

Hopefully my writings will help someone else going through the living hell that PTSD and COVID 19 is for some people, if you are unfortunate enough to catch the virus or suffer from PTSD then you may want to think about keeping a diary, it really does help.

There is so much fear and misinformation out there already I felt writing a book about my experiences couldn't really do any harm; there is no doubt that Corona Virus is a debilitating and cruel disease with no rhyme or reason to it! But after studying the actions of the Government and people of this great country over the last few months it seems to me there is something even more dangerous and cruel; and that is the seeming enjoyment of certain people to spread fear amongst the populace for their own ends.

Whether it comes from the Government scientists, the media or the man in the street, fear; spreads faster than the Corona Virus itself, it undermines happiness, good will, security and well being, not just physical well being but mental wellness and thought processes.

After being in the Armed Forces in a lot of war zones I have learnt to control my fear, not by suppressing it but by channelling the fear into constructive and helpful purpose, I still feel fear now but I have learnt to not let it take over my life, fear impedes human function and rational thought, the 'flight or fight' syndrome, you either stand and fight or you run away.

I am lucky to be able to stand firm and think through the fear and still be able to function, to find a solution; to work a way out; but some people are not so fortunate, seeking out reassurance and comfort from various and sometimes dubious sources.

The Government, the media, the man in the street, the very people then; that can spread the fear in the first place; this in turn makes them very powerful and dangerous people, it makes people with fear reliant on their every word and action; in the Armed Forces we have a doctrine of questioning everything and presume nothing 'presumption is the mother of all fuck ups'

I presumed you bought the ammo! I presumed you did! Ergo we have NO ammo and we are about to go into battle; my advice such as it is for this particular battle against Corona Virus is believe nothing, question everything, and always look in from outside of the box, if after doing all this it still looks like the truth; then it probably is!

Stay safe everybody; we will all laugh about this one day!

****

Part Two

'The Verse'

The Verse - Table of Contents 1:

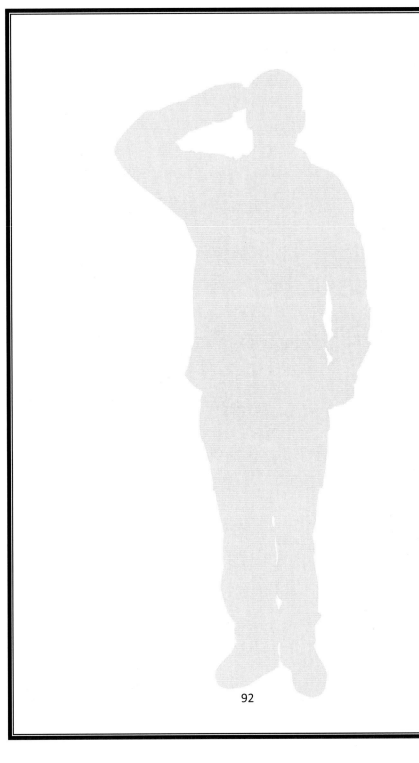

The Verse - Table of Contents 2:

***

The Verse - Table of Contents 3:

****

The Verse - Table of Contents 4:

****

Battlefield

In a field of poppies I bury my head

Because if I look up I will surely be dead

****

The buzzes of rounds zing past my ear

If you just lower your aim I won't be here

****

The crack of the bullet the smell of the fight

I'm hugging the ground with all my might

****

The urge to stand up and flee this scene

Is overtaken by the feeling of anger making me mean

****

I return hard fire and I see a red mist

I watch him fall to the ground with a dying twist

****

I move forward shooting as I go

Using all the skills I now remember I know

****

At last the incoming rounds subside

All around us the enemy have lost and died

****

This fight is not over its barely begun

For tomorrow we will do it all again and shun

****

The fear, the terror we have been taught to suppress

And take the lives of how many is anyone's guess

****

But for now I thank the pretty poppy flower

For hiding me from this vicious metal shower

****

In a Field of Poppies Afghanistan 2008

IED

The flash, the dust, the ground, the air sucked out of me

My hearing comes back to the sound of my brother's plea

****

My brother laying there looks at me in disbelief

His leg has gone – he shakes like a leaf

****

Don't worry my brother I shout to him

I see the tears in his eyes start to well and brim

****

Come on my brother please stay with me

You've only lost your leg below the knee

****

I break out your morphine your pain to quell

And write the 'M' on your forehead for the medic to tell

****

Don't worry my brother I'm here for you

And over my shoulder your body I threw

****

To the rear with you I ran and ran and ran

Through those fields of poppies - that day in Afghan.

****

Through those poppies I ran and ran...

General Horrocks:

Gentlemen this is a story you will tell your grandchildren;

And mightily bored they'll be.

A Bridge Too Far

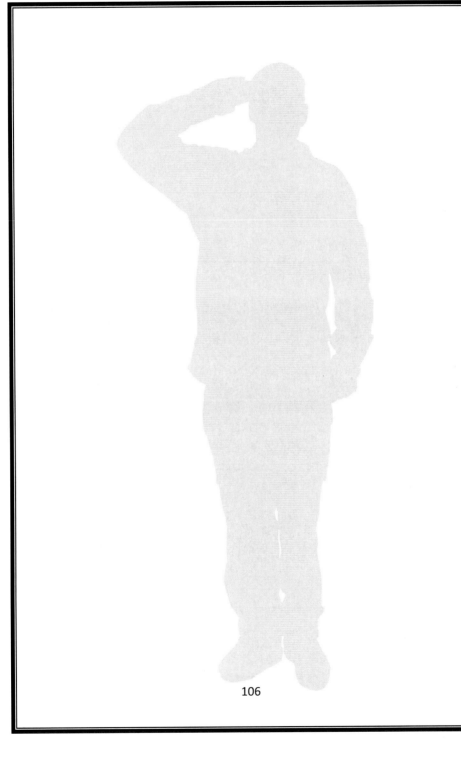

Heroes

Believe in heroes... We aren't that bad

What's left in our heads only makes us sad

****

Our families and friends they try their best

But we have to live with what we detest

****

The killing the death the pointless pain

And all for what? There is no gain

****

One day maybe these feelings will all go away

Until then we hide our stories; cry and pray

****

We join the band of brothers throughout the ages

Who come home hurt, damaged and frightened to turn pages

****

So what's the point in carrying on?

When we think our heads are broken and gone

****

Its times like this we do what we do best

We head for home our loved ones and rest.

****

Colonel Max Radl:

A wink from a pretty girl at a party results rarely in a climax

But a man is a fool not to push a suggestion as far as it will go

The Eagle has Landed

To Serve

No matter how, where or when we serve

We all have a very steep learning curve

****

Brought from all corners of this green land

A suitcase and a rail warrant in our hand

****

It's hard at first to get into our stride

But by the end we are beaming with pride

****

When they cut so short our military hair

We know it all helps when we pass off the square

****

Our uniforms pressed so sharp and clean

The hours spent bulling our boots to make them gleam

****

It all goes to make us who and what we are

And gives us the stories to recount in the bar

****

We travel away from our loved ones and others

But the time we spend with each other makes us brothers

****

To look after each one in time of danger

And lay down our lives (if needed) for a stranger

****

We fight for our country and all that we think true

We fight for each other and people like you

****

So next time you see a uniform of this green and good land

Remember to smile, say thanks, and offer your hand

****

To serve is a privilege and we are proud

And to anyone who will listen we tell them loud

****

We stand up tall and tell our stories

Of our distant battles and past glories

****

When we leave and are at last at rest

We consider ourselves lucky and very blessed

****

To have come this far and out of harm

Where again we can be ourselves and bask in calm

****

So thank you everyone for your love, support and care

Of your sacrifice and thoughts we are well aware

****

It's been hard for you all whilst we were away

But we are now home, safe with you and to stay

****

Three generations of fighting men.

Liam Devlin:

I realised fear one morning, when the blare of the fox hunters sound.

When they are all chasing after the poor bloody fox

It's safer to be dressed like a hound

The Eagle has Landed

Brothers

So here we all are waiting to march

Our chests full of pride and our collars starched

****

Medals all correct and shining so bright

In the heat and emotion it's easy to lose sight

****

We are here for our brothers unreturned

And to remember their sacrifice hard earned

****

So when we march today spare a thought

For our brothers not with us who bravely fought

****

We will always remember the good and the bad

Of the times we spent with our brothers and be glad

****

These times were special just like them

And our feelings and pride, death will not stem

****

So my brothers if you are looking down at us

Remember we will never forget you plus...

****

We will drink and laugh and sing out loud

Remembering our brothers and always proud

****

Brothers in Arms Southern Iraq 2004

Souls

We talk about the men who fought and died in wars time ago

But what about the souls left behind I want to know

****

Battle and blood is hard to forget

The smell the mess and the noise inject...

****

... A fear a sweat that is hard to shake off

We lay in our sweat like water in a trough

****

Bringing it all back when the lights go down and out

Wake screaming and punching and full of shout

****

So where does it all end for us souls returned?

Maybe hanging from a beam at last interned

****

Every year we are forced to admit we are left and still here

Not with our brave brothers laid down asleep and with no fear

****

119

We continue to live with guilt, shame and mad thought

We remember the battles and fights well fought

****

One day we will join our brave brothers in arm

At rest asleep and finally calm

****

History

I'm full of so much history

Yet have an empty soul

****

The years of too much tempo

So sadly take their toll

****

From places long forgotten

To those of yesterday

****

It didn't seem to matter then

All thoughts of death at bay

****

But death has many moments

Its time stamped in your brain

****

The guilt of us survivors

To you might seem insane

****

But yet another facet

At least it seems to me

****

My loss of being in a team

Where death would follow thee

****

I still search for excitement

I want that sudden rush

****

When all around seems chaos

The brain inflicts its hush

****

That feeling you're impregnable

You're there to do your job

****

It's only in these later years

That chaos makes me sob

****

Thanks to K.T. an Apache Helicopter Pilot

Fade Fast

My life fades; but my memories stay clear

The days and nights draw long but I am still here

****

I live my life with people who can never understand

The horrors and pain I've had to deliver with my hand

****

My eyes and my soul seeing lives ebb and fall away

The thoughts of my guilt and shame are here to stay

****

At time the work I did seemed so just and right

And in the heat of the moment all I could do was fight

****

It's the times when I am alone and full of thought

That my world collapses and my mind gets caught

****

Back there again with all the scenes so real

More vivid and colourful; my flashbacks won't heal

****

Our grandfathers never spoke about the horrors of their war

Because people never cared to understand and to ask more

****

So all I have left is the hope my life fades fast

Then I can forever switch off my horrors of past.

****

Mad Marks 'The Road Warrior' ☺

Christmas a time of Fear

Christmas time can be hard for us to bear

At times it looks like we are cruel and don't care

****

But nothing could be further from reality

We just find things unreal and far from your glee

****

Whilst all those around us party and be merry

We remember our brothers in arms we had to bury

****

So at times if we seem a little distracted and aloof

Maybe we are remembering the time we seemed bullet proof

****

Even though we are home and in your safe hands

Our minds cast us further back to those hot lands

****

Where our brothers died and gave us their all

And we learnt to keep our heads further down and crawl

****

It's amazing how it feels when it's you someone's trying to kill

By shooting and bombing your blood they want to spill

****

At times we wonder how the hell we came through

Running through poppy fields the enemy to pursue

****

Then at last to the safety of our RV we came

But bearing the scars of torment and self-blame

****

Again we made it off the field of battle without a scratch

The enemy we caught and fought hard to dispatch

****

So please remember Christmas for us can feel like glue

Always trying hard to wade and force our way through.

****

For you good people Christmas is a time of happiness and great cheer

But for veterans who remember so much it can be a time of great fear.

****

126

Life of Jerry

I see you looking many questions on your lips

Well I'm furry, brown, run fast and love chips

****

My name is Jerry and I am now way past five

I live with my veteran dad and keep him alive

****

I collect his medicine from the cupboard on time

At breakfast, dinner and lunch I climb...

****

...onto his lap I deposit what he needs

So he can carry on with his day and do all his deeds

****

I'm an assistance dog for military personnel

Who have been to war, been hurt and made unwell

****

But with my help my dad gets around

I'm just a cuddly, friendly, loving little hound

****

We have a bond together that will last and last

So please when you see us together walking past

****

Ask my dad if you can touch and distract

As he is relying on me to help him and be exact

****

I wear my red jacket with loyalty and pride

My head held high and proud when I stride

****

I wear my own poppy its purple you see

It was awarded for courage and service to me

****

I, like my dad wear my poppy with pride

To remember and respect all the people that died

****

So thank you for looking and wanting to learn

About what I do during my day and why I can look stern

****

Now I must dash off ... duty calls

My dad's promised me a walk and a game with balls

****

Jerry 'A clever lad'

A very special Dad and Daughter moment!

Inspired

I am so inspired to help others its true

But there always seems so many not few

****

I strive to do one thing the best I can

And not many things badly for my fellow man

****

With my four legged friend and confident hound

Our care for fellow veterans knows no bound

****

We strive to be there to help where we can

Our veterans from Iraq; Falklands and Afghan

****

The horrors we have seen will never go away

But our own brand of humour and love will outweigh

****

The rough times and hard we have to go through

To make some sense of it all and be with you

****

If we can all do just a little bit more our veterans to save

It will make our day better by helping our brave

****

Sometimes it's hard for me to express my thought

So I've taken to writing them down to stop getting fraught

****

I get so frustrated by the way we treat our vets

Homeless; penniless but that's not as bad as it gets

****

They all gave so much so you can live out of harm

And go about your daily lives and be in peace and calm

****

No matter how hard we try we cannot do it all alone

Even with my special dog Jerry who only needs a bone

****

So please try and help us to deliver what veterans need

And spare some time and thought without them having to plead

****

Some of them suffer with physical wounds and scars

Many of us succumb to our own mental memoirs

****

So take the inspiration and help some of us out

We will appreciate all you can do for us; of that there is no doubt.

****

Animal Partnership Award

Honouring the unique relationships and companionship provided by animals, and/or the achievements of individuals or organisations engaged with animals, that support and/or empower members of the Armed Forces Community.

Award Sponsors
2014, 2015,
2016, 2017,
2018, 2019
& 2020

pets
at home

where pets come first

Service Dogs UK:
Mark Lanchbery & Jerry
Winner 2018

@SoldierOnAwards   SoldieringOnAwards   #SOA2020   @soldieringonawards

A wonderful and humbling moment

134

BUCKINGHAM PALACE

15th July 2019

Dear Mr Mallett,

The Queen wishes me to write and thank you for your recent letter in which you tell Her Majesty about the courage and commitment of a former soldier, Mr Mark Lanchbery.

The Queen was very interested to learn of your friend's outstanding efforts to help other Army veterans through his work as a mentor for the charity, 'Service Dogs UK', along with his Assistance Dog, Jerry.

Her Majesty was moved by your warm tribute to Mr Lanchbery, whose constant positivity and happy attitude is a major source of comfort to others in trouble, despite suffering his own difficulties and extreme pain on a daily basis.

The Queen would be glad if you would convey her good wishes and thanks to Mr Lanchbery for the kind and effective assistance he offers to injured service personnel, and I am to thank you once again for your thought in writing to tell Her Majesty about this very special person whom you are so proud to know.

Yours sincerely,

Richenda Elton

Lady-in-Waiting

Another amazing moment!

Light

Thank you to everyone for coming to our awards night

We have spent months and months trying to get our training right

****

And now with our dogs we stand rightly proud

Here tonight before a daunting crowd

****

Months ago we would have never stood here and done this

In fact in military speak 'we would have given it a miss'

****

Your support has given us new strength and pride

With our trained assistance dogs now rightly by our side

****

When we first started the goals seemed a million miles away

But with our trainers help we were committed and here to stay

****

We battled on; the training at times could be long and tough

But not as bad as the nights we spent alone, they were rough

****

The light at the end of the tunnel was shining so bright

So we had to put our heads down and go for the light

****

Week after week we attended and put in the hard graft

Sometimes our trainee assistance dogs were our only life raft

****

So now after our journey we have come out into the light

Having an assistance dog next to you somehow seems right

****

We have got all of you here to be grateful for

For your support, dedication, love and more

****

So when you see us walking down the street a spring in our stride

Just remember all of you put us there and gave us back our pride

****

My brothers and I cannot thank you all enough

For continuing to be there for us when times get tough

****

Now it's time to sign off before the tears start to flow

Because we're not very good with emotion; you know

****

Plus my wonderful little Jerry is bored and looking at me

I promised him, if he was good, a juicy sausage for his tea

****

140

Our Poppy

A pity our country no longer breeds men of true guts and pride

It seem many men when called to arms go and hide

****

Leaving the few and hearty to go and fight

And stand up for our England and all that is right

****

So mock the poppy if you feel that is just

But remember this is our country and protect it we must

****

Fight for all that is left of our good and green land

Just remember as veterans of this great nation we will still stand

****

So if you have the misfortune to come across one of us out and about

Abuse our poppy but expect a big clout

****

No good being PC of softly, softly here

We don't give a fuck about your bleating, moaning and tear

****

141

So if you want our respect and to live in harmony with us

Then give us our moment, embrace our poppy, our values and fuss!

****

Remember our sacrifice...

... And remember our pride

Machines

We watch them return all battered scarred and bent

They are the victims of war just as the soldiers we sent

****

They protect and transport us in our time of our need

Keep us safe and ready to fight with machine guns to feed

****

The wheels and the tracks rumble across terrain so rough

Made of steel and armoured plate so really made tough

****

These are the latest of our fighting machines to go to war

Which help us defeat the enemy and make kills to score?

****

So when you feel like cursing the hot metal, sharp edges and heat

Just remember these machines save you and your feet

****

So next time you see them roll battered through the camp gates

Just remember all they've done to save you and your mates.

****

Battered, Scarred and Bent.

Pilgrims

£82000 missing pounds I hear you cry

Stolen from wounded and brave servicemen; I sigh!

****

It seems you can take what you want nowaday

And get away with it by saying gone bust; no cash; no way

****

Robbed of flights to send the pilgrims on tour

And at the last minute having to struggle to raise more

****

What you have done is so bloody bad

You make our blood boil; feel aggrieved and very sad

****

We hope you get all you got coming and deserve

But we know you will try to swing; duck; avoid and swerve

****

No doubt in today's world of snowflakes and politically correct

Punishment will not come even though you're number one suspect

****

Do the right thing Black Tip Travel and send our money back to us?

We could have helped so many of Britain's few without fuss

****

We are a charity and rely on people of this country to be generous

Not have their money stolen by sharks like you in waters treacherous

****

Do not make the mistake of taking us for wounded and weak

We will always be strong; forceful; brave and full of speak

****

So come on Black Tip Travel make us again smile

Do the decent and right thing and return our pile.

****

We are the Pilgrims, master; we shall go
Always a little further: it may be
Beyond that last Fr mou i ba red with snow
Across th gry limmering sea

Somewhere quiet!

Laugh

I had to laugh to myself the other day

When I watched civilians like ants in a melee.

****

Sometimes it's hard to feel any concern

When you've watched your friend blown up and start to burn.

****

So what seems like big problems to you?

Think of us struggling and wearing our shoe

****

We do things differently because of what we've seen

And we try really hard not to be so mean

****

We have our problems; thoughts and fears

So don't feel so bad about us when you see us in tears

****

The things we have seen will stay with us its true

But with your help and love we will get through

****

So if you see us one day laugh and smile

It's because we love watching ants like you run your busy daily mile

****

Winston Churchill

Now this is not the end. It is not even the beginning of the end. But it is perhaps, the end of the beginning.

Battle of Britain 1940

Jigsaw

A part of the jigsaw that is me is left over there

A feeling of loss, pain and incomplete despair

****

It's not my warm blood soaking into the hot sand

Or the deep eyes of the medic holding my hand

****

Or the euphoria of the morphine as its blots out the pain

Or the morphine dreams of riding a white charger across the plain

****

It's an indescribable wish and I yearn to go back and see

Where some of my life and fun was sucked out of me

****

I've tried so hard to return from war and be as I once was

It's as if the sands of time have got into my blood because;

****

All I feel is incomplete, half here, empty and alone

The call of the desert and the sky full of stars is in my bones

****

So when the morphine wears off and the surgeons repair

There's a piece of my jigsaw in despair left over there.

****

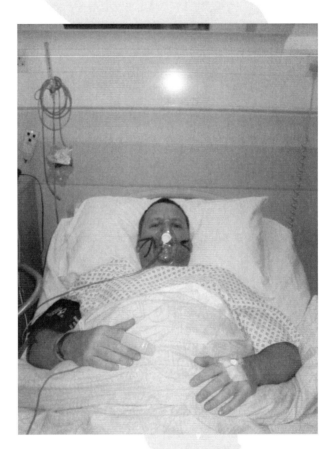

Left in despair in 2008.

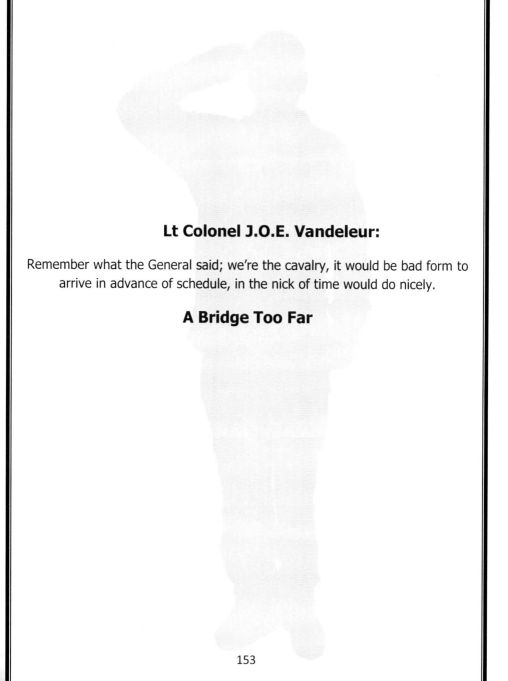

Lt Colonel J.O.E. Vandeleur:

Remember what the General said; we're the cavalry, it would be bad form to arrive in advance of schedule, in the nick of time would do nicely.

A Bridge Too Far

Be the Best

They say join the Army and be the best

But when we go to war we face the ultimate test

****

Are we men who stand brave, firm and fight

Or do we give in to our fears and leave full flight

****

This is an Army of volunteers and we serve our country true

We fight for our flag, our people and yes; you

****

We see things that no men should see and a lifetime of pain

We lay our lives on the line to protect and not for gain

****

So when we come home we need time and peace to reflect

About the horrors we have seen and try hard to eject

****

Some of us will never walk or think the same way

The memories of our comrades always in our minds will stay

****

So we can hold our heads up high and know we've passed the test

We served in our British Army and we were the best.

****

Being 'The Best'

Chinook

I hear the sound of the Chinook coming for me

The dust makes sure that I cannot see

****

I feel the medic working fast and doing his stuff

Come on mate it bloody hurts; so don't be so rough

****

I feel a mixture of calm, fear, excitement and pain

The morphine courses through me; liquid through my vein

****

But now the feeling of warmth starts to flow through

The morphine takes over my desire to panic and spew

****

I am lifted and pulled this way and that

To get me away quickly from this mortal combat

****

I finally get to see the blades turning slow above me

And to hear the engines howling like a banshee

****

I get the feeling of flying fast through the air

Is this really real? Am I really there?

****

The questions flow free now that the pain has gone

The sounds of the rotors keep on and keep on

****

Finally I fall sleep in a morphine induced sea

That day I heard the Chinook coming just for me.

****

A Chinook in Iraq doing what they do best!

Contact

Contact right! Contact right!

Come on lads get in the fight

****

The sounds of war buzz from the trees

The smell of war wafts in on the breeze

****

We are in the thick of our bullet and battle

You can hear the machine guns cough and rattle

****

The spit of hot lead flying through the air

We run forward into battle without a care

****

The sweat and dust gets into your eyes

Aiming for the tree line that's our prize

****

To take on the enemy and fight to win

The anger and frustration gets under your skin

****

But here we are now in the thick of the fight

That day in Afghanistan on our 'contact right'

****

Dreams

Every boyhood dream was made very real for me one day

When I was placed on a mercy flight crew to travel far away

****

To fly from somewhere in the United States to the jungles of Belize

To save our SB brothers in the jungle from the ravages of the seas

****

We climbed aboard the C130 and were manifested as a mercy flight crew

Threw on our medical kit, shown our maggot space and where to go to the loo

****

The taxi down the runway and take off was uneventful very smooth, and sure

We had every confidence in our special crew to take us there and more

****

We flew on and on to the drone whiling away the hours and the time

By playing cards, checking weapons and listening to the cockpit chime

****

Flying over the deep blue sea and looking down at islands below

Sometimes low under the radar so our journey wouldn't show

****

Hurricane Katrina had landed, been, destroyed, flooded and gone

And now hurricane Rita was on its way to threaten and to us bear on

****

Our boys in the jungle would not stand a chance to survive

So everyone was waiting on the tarmac for our flight to arrive

****

We flew high and above hurricane Rita on its way in

All the cloud formations were whipped up tight and in a spin

****

We could see from up high the chaos and the eye of the storm

The violence and destruction were starting to form

****

The flight came in heavy and fast as the winds were howling now

This was going to be a fast in and out there was no time to allow...

****

For greetings and niceties, we needed to be in and out fast

And back up to the safety of altitude and away from danger at last

****

The pallets of kit were loaded on, along with all the men

Strapped down at last secure and ready to take off when...

****

Out of the blue there's a big shout, you old bastard what are you doing here?

And there stands tall and unshaven one of the DS grinning from ear to ear

****

It's an old mate from my long ago past, looking tanned and very lean

What me? I ask smiling back, I'm just living out my boyhood dream

****

Frontline

The life of a frontline soldier is a lonely place

No one at home will ever understand the pace

****

The constant fear and readiness of injury or even death

Never knowing when you will draw your last and final breath

****

The mind constantly checks every scenario and backup plan

The eyes of the mind fully open to digest and set to scan

****

Looking out for anything that could do us harm

Being the first to make ready and sound the alarm

****

When the hate and violence finally starts to come

It's almost a relief to let yourself go and give it some

****

You almost wish it would happen to unwind your stomachs coil

Before the stress takes over and your mind starts to boil

****

So when you see the frontline soldier locked in his lonely place

Its best to let him unwind be quiet and have his own space.

****

The Frontline.

Guns and Grins

Welcome to the jungle we all loudly sing

Flying across the desert in our rotor wing

****

Making good progress flying low and fast

This is the fun in war that will never ever last

****

But for now thanks to our mad American friends

And a Black Hawk Helicopter we hope it never ends

****

We sit in the side pods M60s loaded and ready to hand

Ready to brass up any trouble coming up from the sand

****

But this flight will be fast, low and combat free

Giving us both time to breathe and be you and me

****

We look at each other and smiles break into grins

We couldn't make this shit up for all our sins

****

At the top of our voices we continue to sing

Welcome to the jungle in 'our' rotor wing

****

Welcome to the Jungle; Black Hawk Style!

Incoming

We sleep below a mountain, safe dug in here

Dreaming of fish and chips and a dewy cold beer

****

Then awoken by the sound of a mortars crash

The dull 'plop' down the tube followed by the smash

****

Someone screams out 'incoming round'

It smashes in again, but we are not found

****

The smoke lies in layers trapped in the morning air

We peer out of our cover and through binoculars stare

****

The rounds keep coming landing quite a way off

It makes us look at each other shrug and almost scoff

****

The lack of being 'bracketed' tells us more

These guys are not experts or very sure...

****

...of the correct procedures or to aim and make it count

And spoil our beautiful morning dug in below that mount.

****

With the Sunrise the Mortars came.

Mary Thelma Bosley

I'm attending a sad memorial today from way long past

To pay respects to my friends mum who was killed in a blast

****

A bad day at the 16th Parachute Brigade in February 1972

Where an IRA car bomb was driven, planted and blew

****

My friends mum worked in the airborne officer's block

At 12.20 that day the ground in Aldershot would rock

****

To the sound of a car bomb designed to maim and kill

And for my friends mum her innocent blood to spill

****

That left my good friend and his brother's orphans to roam

And in the family of the Parachute Regiment to find a home

****

It's been 47 years but the pain is still clear and very raw

And some sense of this act we all still try to claw

****

But every year we will attend to make our memories last

To not forget all those poor brave mums killed in that blast.

****

The Memorial to the 1972 Bombing of the 16th Parachute Brigade Officers Mess in Aldershot by the IRA.

We will never forget.

Nasher

Asleep dreaming safe in our beds we snoozed

Awoken by mortars coming in now I'm dazed and confused

****

I lay there listening not sure if I heard right

I could've been dreaming and woken up in a fright

****

Sure enough the next round came closer then the last

Come on get up, weapon ready and get dressed fast

****

The next one landed and the building creaked and shook

And out of the wall my air con unit it took

****

Nasher mate are you ok? That was fucking close!

You stay there bruv you call back, I will see what goes

****

I open my door to see you standing there

Flip flops; pants; weapon but otherwise bare!

****

What the fuck Nash you cannot fight them like that

Before you take the fuckers on at least wear ya hat

****

Despite the danger it's hard to not laugh and smile

At the near naked fat bloke all ready and hostile

****

The enemy mortars faded as soon as they came

Just another episode launched in this deadly game

****

So for now we will all go back to our warm and safe beds

And catch up on our dreams of home and some zzzzzds.

The little fat bloke (on the right) in 2018.

Bruvafromanothermuffa by Nasher

It doesn't matter when you see him

He's always very near

You wake up early hours in a sweat

But he's there to lend you an ear

****

He won't moddycuddle you and tell you it's alright

But he will stand (short) by your side and help you win the fight

****

Sometimes you want to bitch slap him

For being a complete and utter twat

But then he will do something stupid

And you almost piss your pants and that

****

Those of us who have had a bruvafromanothermuffa

Have been through thick and thin

You know it's a special kind of love if you will

But never looked at as a sin

****

We have had each other's backs at times

But will also stand toe to toe

We hope for a peaceful sleep at the end of the day

While we bid farewell to our foe.

The Brothers 'captured' T34

Op Banner

The Northern Ireland legacy again rears its ugly head

Isn't it better for everybody to put all this hate to bed?

****

Instead of re-igniting bitter rivalry and good people divide

We should be working together to all live at last on one side

****

Mistakes and atrocities were committed that's very sad and true

Bloody Sunday, Warren Point, and the Aldershot bomb in 72

****

Stupid people and groups fan the fire for their own wicked gain

And hoist the flag of terrorism to justify people's pain

****

47 years on and they are still using the hate and harm

To spoil the lives of many and spread the fear and alarm

****

Do we really want to go back to the far off bad old days?

Or do we put the past in the past and forever there it stays

****

So it's time to end the blame and put this legacy to bed

Before the senseless violence and killing again rears its head

****

Rendezvous

Sat amongst the rubble floor

A silence I'd not known

My world inside another world

This time for me alone

****

With no idea of what nor why

My time just has no place

I cannot move eyes from the floor

I sit in deaths embrace

****

No warmth, no cold, nor even wind

For nothing moving here

I've no idea if I'm alive

My long lost mortal fear

****

Thanks to K.T. an Apache Helicopter Pilot

Resupply

Across the desert in our loaded WMIK we drove, brothers in arms

The heat, the dust, the flatness and devoid of covering palms

****

Our grandfathers fought and died here many desert moons ago

But their war was different against a true, gallant and proud foe

****

Looking all around at the sand billiard table, but without the balls

It is hard to imagine any sense of chance; just a lot of close calls

****

We continue to drive feeling more and more exposed and alone

But confident in the strength of each other in this our combat zone

****

Now's the time to stop, eat, brew and take in the dark cold night

And to set ourselves up for welcoming our weekly resupply flight

****

This brave flight would bring us our news, water, ammunition and food

To last us another week on our journey into this land and raise our mood

****

The sound of the silence is broken by the encryption crackling into life

And a big machine flies low over our position, its wings like a knife...

****

Cut through the cold desert air its night vision eyes all seeing what's below?

We snap our Infra Red cylumes and shake them to make them glow

****

The big machine lands and we feel the prop blast kicking up sand and dust

The ramp goes down and we see the loadie inviting us in through the thrust

****

Up the ramp we go to unload the tools of our trade and what we need

The big black machine needs to get out quick; the props are up to speed

****

We grab our kit and go and with a wave from the loadies cylumed hand

Once more the big machine kicks up the dust and leaves us alone in the sand

****

The silence and calm once more envelopes us on this cold and dark night

Leaving us with our thoughts and fears about when we will have to fight

****

As we snuggle down into our sleeping bags leaving our brothers above with their night eye

We dream of big black machines hopefully taking us home; on the very next resupply

****

The Resupply

Riot

We stand facing the riot trying to look hard and tall

Despite all the gear I felt really exposed and small

****

The bricks came in and bounced off my shield

We stood together and strong we weren't going to yield

****

This just made the crowd angrier and begin to shout

One man ran in; a good target for my baton to clout

****

I heard his collarbone crack and give under my blow

He stopped dead for a moment then had another go

****

I hit him again; about the head just to make sure

He bounced off my shield and slid to the floor

****

The crowd pushed forward with hate in their eyes

It's us they want to hurt; smash and despise

****

We stand firm and with our batons our shields start to drum

Beating up a rhythm to a crescendo and then some

****

We move forward pushing and hitting as we go

The bricks and bottles and violence start's to flow

****

We push the crowd back and they start to run

We continue on forward our job here nearly done

****

That day at the riot when I felt so insignificant and small

Ended with me defeating my fear and feeling 6 feet tall

****

RPG

I hear the shout go out RPG!

I look up and see the trail fly over me

****

I dive for the ground and hit it so hard

That was close, they had marked my card

****

It impacts the wall way behind my head

The shrapnel spreads out looking for me to shred

****

We all lay there on hold, our senses extreme

Looking and hunting the threat to our team

****

The silence is deafening, a cliché I know

The crackle of spite and gunfire joins the show

****

The rounds pass close like an angry bee

Aimed and sure searching for me

****

Someone calls out, 'keep your head's well down'

There's no point in helping this Taliban clown

****

At last the firing stops and the enemy melt away

Saving the fight to take our lives another day

****

Incoming!

The Long and Short

The difference between the long and the short

Is with the long you will never get caught...

****

Out; having to use your short at close quarter

Because the range on the short is by far much shorter

****

It's always better to use your long for far out

For keeping the enemy away and in no doubt

****

You will place your rounds sure, long and true

This will make things safer for you and your crew

****

So remember the long belongs tight in the shoulder

Whilst the short is better off kept in the holster

****

Bear in mind the enemy is best kept out far with the long

If you have to draw and use your short it's probably gone wrong

****

So; the long and the short now hopefully you've got the gist

Are there any questions or anything you might have missed?

****

The Long...

... And the Short

The Patrol

The feeling in my guts outwardly gives nothing away

Of the apprehension of going on yet another patrol today

****

All the equipment and weapons systems double checked yet again

Keeping busy and alert this way seems to keep me sane

****

For we are going out from relative safety into mortal danger

To put ourselves on the line and into the sights of a stranger

****

The hardest part about being on patrol and in harm's way

Is realising it's you the enemy want to kill and slay

****

But take a deep breath; keep calm and be stoic we should

And stand by our friends; comrades and brotherhood

****

For today our mission will be completed and will not fail

As once more into the jaws of death we taunt and sail

****

As we the patrol using all the skills that were so hard to learn

Seeking out the enemy in his territory, danger around every turn

****

The sun beats relentlessly down and the ground is rough

But we are proud British soldiers and built of stern stuff

****

But today our patrol will be peaceful and totally event free

So we can all go back to camp for a nice cup of tea

****

As we walk through the camp gates my gut starts to unwind

All the feeling of apprehension and tension left way behind

****

It's almost euphoric this sense of well being; safety and joy

But tomorrows another day for us the Taliban to poke and annoy.

The Patrol

Tracer

The line of tracer heads away from me

One round in every five from my GPMG

****

Lighting up my target for others to place

Sending death right into the Taliban's space

****

The belt of brass is fed in from the left

And spits out lead and ultimately death

****

The beat of the gun is somehow in rhyme

It's going to get you Terry in double quick time

****

I watch the rounds chop down his defence

He would cut and run if he had any sense

****

But this is not the Taliban's way

He's going to stay and fight and die today

****

He continues to fire and show us he's brave

But against all odds he's going to his grave

****

At last the firing slows down and stops

And with his last breath and blood he drops

****

My line of tracer has done its job for me

With a tick tick the barrel cools down; on my GPMG

****

The Special Soldier

Britain has a special son, his skills are world renowned

Tensions around the globe erupt; he's the first upon the ground

****

He's the lion of the army, to this most would agree

He's the fully rounded soldier that many want to be

****

Though plenty seek selection, few ever make the grade

The sandy beret signifies; a master of his trade

****

He's a military specialist, an expert with his tools

He's quick to speak what's on his mind and doesn't suffer fools

****

He's a stubborn sort of fellow who seems without a care

His motto's not for cowards, to win he has to dare

****

You'll find him in the jungles, the deserts and the snow

But ask him where he will be next week; he'll say he doesn't know

****

He moves freely in the daytime but always out of sight

He appears where least expected and a phantom in the night

****

He'll face extreme conditions with a minimum supply

His body may be soaking, but his humours always dry

****

He pays the price for liberty, far from the warmth of home

His family pays a price as well, through endless months alone

****

In public celebrations we never see his face

In times of recognition he feels quite out of place

****

He says it's just his duty; the service that he vowed

But England thanks you anyway; you've done this country proud.

****

In memory of the fallen 21 – 22 - 23

Life isn't so bad!

I sit in my quiet garden and soak up the hot sun

NO body armour, NO helmet and for sure NO gun

****

A good meal in my belly, no more service rations for me

I eat slow and dignified now and sip my cup of tea

****

A warm soft bed instead of the hard dirty floor

NO one eye open, NO enemy at the door

****

This civvies life, you know it isn't too bad

But I miss my brothers and that makes me sad

****

NO more war for me, my fighting is all done

So now I can just sit in my garden and soak up some sun!

****

Written May 2020

The Beauty of the Sun; May 2020

A Few Good Men

Cimic house Al Amarah and a few good men

Held back the bastard hordes of hundreds and ten

****

Day and night they attacked to oust us out

Barely an hour went by when up went the shout

****

Here the hundreds come again stand to! Stand to!

Give them the hell their asking for boys and as if on cue

****

Everyone opened up with everything they had

To get rid of the fear and aggression we were glad

****

We fought real hard to keep the hordes away

Followed armed men with our sights and blew them away

****

The red mist in our brains converted calmly to shoot

And see the pink mist at the end of our bullets route

****

That told us we were calm calculated and exact

To follow the path of our bullet to point of impact

****

Again and again we watched the enemy drop

But more and more came it never seemed to stop

****

The heat and sweat and noise of battle

The smoke and fire and the machine guns rattle

****

On and on we defended our brother's lives to live

This drained every ounce until we had no more to give

****

It may have just been an old governor's house to you

But for the defenders of Cimic it was a symbol in lieu

****

Of the making of legends and a few good men

For people to remember the battles of Cimic way back then

****

Bollocks

Being made to wonder if going to war and fighting was worth while

For a country that is ours; far divided, toxic and no longer able to smile

****

Smile about the daft and silly things and the odd politically incorrect joke

Now frightened to say anything to cause offence with words lightly spoke

****

This great and proud country used to thrive on sense of humour and grin

Now the politicians use political correctness to chuck out rhetoric and spin

****

In almost every word they speak; utter bollocks comes to mind

It's getting harder in what they say for the truth and sense to find

****

So when I think of myself and my brothers going off to fight another war

It's no wonder we are struggling to find good reason to be there and more

****

So I guess we do it for ourselves our brothers and families; to go the extra mile

I guess we will just have to wait for our country to fix itself and again start to smile

****

Charlie

I sit in my quiet, safe English garden drinking a dewy cold beer

Remembering my time in conflict and my best friend not here

****

It all seems a lifetime away now and mentally as clear as mud

The time I cleaned my friends watch to wash away the blood

****

To sanitise and send home his personal effects to his family dear

I often sit and think of Charlie and his family shedding a tear

****

That memory will never leave me I guess it's ingrained in my soul

The comical soldier that was Charlie died and left a massive hole

****

Spilling his warm blood and taking his last breath on the deserts hot sand

And in the quiet of death he rose up to Valhalla and Samarkand

****

Flying high on the back of Pegasus through the high fluffy cloud

If I listen carefully I can hear you screaming in excitement; very loud

****

So my friend Charlie you are not forgotten but very much still here

And I raise my glass to the cloud and you my friend; and drink my cold beer

****

The Golden Road to Samarkand

We travel not for trafficking alone;
by hotter winds our fiery hearts are fanned:
For lust of knowing what should not be known
we take the Golden Road to Samarkand.

James Elroy Flecker

210

Covenant

The Armed Forces Covenant! What the fuck is that supposed to be?

On returning home wounded and hurt; it's done fuck all for me!

****

Dumped on the NHS as the military was unable to cope

All the military hospitals and facilities sold off by some government dope!

****

Abandoned in a system that has no idea of military life or clue

Of how to help military personnel; so get to the back of the queue

****

We don't need to be told to get out of bed or make ourselves smart

Or need sympathy or our arses wiped; or a bleeding heart

****

What we need is a covenant that will do what it says on the tin

Not some politician that's going to fuck us over in the name of spin

****

We volunteered to do our countries dirty deeds without question

All we got in return after 6 months was a week's 'decompression'

****

Landing in Cyprus to get pissed up and fight amongst ourselves

And then sent home damaged and put up high upon the shelves

****

Until the next time when we are needed to do your dirty work

If we had any sense we would tell you to fuck yourselves and shirk

****

But this is not the proud and brave British Soldiers way

From the true allegiance to our Queen we will never sway

****

Some people will say we are soldiers that's what we do go and 'fight'

And to stop bloody moaning and just get out of fuckiing sight

****

We understand this; there is something right in what you say

But then don't fucking tell us we have a covenant and then snatch it away

****

Govern! My Arse!

The scapegoats in government are dropping like flies

But one day there will be no one left to hide all your lies

****

You need to start telling the truth to turn the tide

Before you are the only one left with nowhere to hide

****

We are all left with a legacy that nobody wants

And a government with no wisdom and no known fonts...

****

...of knowledge and answers to draw upon

All manner of truth, sense and pride has gone

****

Year after year you have destroyed our country true

And now we are left with the dregs; and of course you!

****

It's too late for you to bleat and lie your way out of this

So when I bend over it's my arse you can kiss

****

Resign; resign we say and do it before it's too late

Before you turn the people of this country to anarchy and hate

****

When it comes it will be the falling in of the skies

And all down to you and your blatant deceit and lies.

****

March 2020

Humility

Hurricane Katrina came to Louisiana USA and left its pain

British troops sent there to help clear up the mess and shame

****

Looters were rife so we were told shoot to kill on sight

Desperate hours, crazy times and us alone to do what's right

****

To defend and help in a way that only British troops know how

And once again show the world we are still the best; even now

****

Whilst parked in a quiet wood after the waters had flowed away

We could hear the animals forced to flee to high ground and they...

****

Were forced together for survival to live in harmony and peace

Whilst they waited for the storm to pass and the winds to cease

****

Sitting there in the silence I had time to think and reflect

If we could all just get along together it would all be so perfect

****

But for now it was time to move on again and do our job

I turned the key in the Hum Vee dash and twisted the knob

****

The engine started and clattered into life, noise and smoke

And away we drove to another location to help other folk

****

As I drove away I thought a bit and said a little prayer

Hoping that the animals were safe, the ones that we left there

****

Animals had grouped together to keep each other from harm

Lessons can be learnt from them, they had a certain charm

****

Being a soldier is not all about being tough and giving pain...

It's about learning to hold your head high and not hang it in shame

****

Humility

After Katrina came us... poor sods ☺

Jihadi Bride

People of Britain you really must understand

We veterans of this great country and land

****

Hang our heads in shame, surprise and fear

Of watching our country be confused and unclear

****

Politicians they forget the sacrifice and lives voluntarily gave

So they can look politically correct, intelligent and brave

****

In the face of the enemy we fought hard and some died

And now you think about bringing home a jihadi bride?

****

Let's make our feelings clear and well understood

We don't want you living here and if we could

****

We would make sure you stay in the place you call hell

And live in the bosom of your jihadi terror cell

****

You have lived there watching beheadings for nearly 4 years

And by your own admission you didn't shed any tears

****

Well now it's your time to cry little jihadi bride

You will not be coming to our country with your crimes to hide

****

At last someone in our government has shown a back bone

And realised letting you into our country would have blown

****

Any chance they would have had of looking at all in control

And fading forever into a political black hole

****

So make no mistake Mr Javid it's with you we all stand

And thank you from the veterans of this great country and land

****

Lost

All the fun and laughter has fucked off and gone from me

And now I'm just an empty shell, a shadow without glee

****

Left by the bastards in establishment to crash and burn

And a sorry story of trust I've had but been forced to unlearn

****

To trust in my army and my government I was a fucking fool

Now that I'm broken I'm no longer a machine; a killing tool

****

For them to use as a soldier to go and maim and kill

And in the name of Great Britain others blood to spill

****

I am just fucking sat here using drink to make myself numb

To forget all the horrors I've seen and to loneliness succumb

****

It's not that I'm sad or regret what I've done and where I've been

Or even the mind numbing atrocities in the name of peace I've seen

****

It's the complete indifference shown by my fellow countryman true

And the lack of understanding and care fucking shown by yes **YOU!**

****

So I lose myself in loneliness and drink to numb the fucking pain

Of being left with my nightmares and thoughts etched in my brain

****

I look at the madness of the world and slowly shake my head

Surely the lies and rhetoric couldn't get more blatant I've said

****

When all around me simply couldn't seem or get any worse

I'm left with an eternal nightmare that in my mind is a curse

****

So when you look at me and wonder where all the fun is at...

Just remember what I fucking fought for and lost in combat

****

Outcast

The feeling of being an outcast rears its monstrous ugly head

Feeling nobody cares about me inside or my mates being dead

****

In your world you rely on social media; made up drama and lies

When I have lost all that is precious to me and now have no ties

****

This is the way of life for most people that really do not care

I feel what's the point of going on and I feel deep pain and despair

****

I fought hard and lost my health and sanity to protect the ones I love

But when it was all over they turn their backs on me and shove

****

To get me away from their world as far as they can push and sweep

They do not want to be reminded of my battered head and shell; I weep

****

What hurts me most and I find hard to understand, grasp and take

Is I really do my best to be the same and a good man again make

****

But you are not the same person they all cry out, rant and scream

You try and be the same person; living a nightmare not a dream

****

My inner eyes will forever see the horrors of war and pain

I'm beginning to realise your right I will never again be sane

****

So where am I left? In a barren land deep inside my head

So maybe it's time for me to join my mates and be better off dead

****

PC or not to be

Whether your politically correct or no

The truth has got to be let out and told so...

****

...we can at last leave the bastard money pit EU

And take back control of our great country and review

****

We have all had enough of being pushed around and told

So let's do what the referendum majority have polled

****

To destroy our values and democracy would be a crime

We would all land on our feet given the opportunity and time

****

Not fall apart and sink into the abyss like many expected

But rise up again as great, strong and respected

****

So when the weak and spineless snowflakes shout about being PC

Revelling in all this confusion and rubbing their hands with glee

****

Ask yourself the question why they want to divide us and distract

Is it to hide their wrongs and misdemeanours and avoid being sacked

****

It cannot be to help this once great country and keep it on the go

Or perhaps being PC to Brussels is more important than saying NO

****

Soldier 'F'

The persecution and trial of brave soldier 'F' designate

Used to relight, refuel the troubles and inflame the hate

****

For the ends and face of the politicians to make them look so good

With no thought or care for soldiers just doing the best they could

****

To be hounded and trawled through the courts in a useless display

To make up for a gross lack of leadership by our government we say

****

So we stand by soldier 'F' and we all stand tall and proud

To be alongside our brother again and shout very loud

****

You will not ever take us down for your own political gain

We will rise up and fight; and fight for justice again

****

Picking on one man for the wrongs you sent us to do

We never saw you on the front line wearing our shoe

****

The people are seeing and turning against you at last to fight

So draw a line to your wrongs of past and make them right

****

We are proud to have served our country we brave and we few

And the strength of our feeling should mean something to you

****

We wonder and wait when one day they will be coming for us

It really could happen; if some fucking snowflakes make a fuss

****

In a country of politically correct and constant apology and blame

Any one of us could end up like soldier 'F' a scapegoat the same

****

So one more British soldier would be skinned and hung out to dry

While the rest of us look on and wonder the hell out of why?

****

You've seen rolling thunder that should have given you a clue

How far we are prepared to go to make sure we persecute you

****

We will always stand alongside our brave brother and mate

When you dare and try prosecuting soldier 'F' designate

****

In memory of the fallen; I – II – III – IV - X

230

Top White

Sanctuary is to be found in Hook in the most unlikeliest place

Where you can be amongst friends and still have your own space

****

Space to unwind, be yourself; where you can be at your ease

Where the hardworking staff do their very best to please

****

When all around you there is madness, uncertainty, confusion and fear

This is a place where you are always welcome and can enjoy your beer

****

When you've been away on operations or just had a gut full at work

You can come to this place, relax, chill out, laugh and shirk

****

The aches and grinds of the day and the madness of the world

You can get peace, quiet and friends here and your mind unfurled

****

This place is well known to those who care about their friends and support

It's a place to come for good food and beer and of course great sport

****

Inside there is a community that thrives and is very rightly proud

So why don't you come and find out yourself and join the crowd

****

You will be made welcome from the minute you walk through the door

And of great service and a friendly happy face you can be sure

****

So where is this sanctuary in Hook? Where to look do I start?

Well look no further my friend, welcome to the Old White Hart

****

Trump or Dump

The ideals and dreams of president elect Trump

Give all the PC snowflakes of America the hump

****

Elected to make America great once again

Did people expect this to happen with no pain?

****

Even a small glance at the bigger picture by you

Will open you mind to see that Trump is being true

****

True to his great people, his great country and beliefs

To build a better place for Americans again to be chiefs...

****

...of their own country to work hard and do well

And to once again be proud of their country and make chests swell

****

Immigration is a problem of that lets be in no doubt

But yet again the politically correct scream holler and shout

****

What about the immigrants' rights they loudly moan

But what about the rights of Americans worked to the bone?

****

Surely Americans come first in their own great land

Land they fought hard to gain, protect and make grand

****

So before you criticise and shout down your President elect

Just remember he's doing his best for your country to protect

****

When you disagree with the ideals and dreams of President Trump

Just be careful your country doesn't end up an immigrant dump

****

Written 2019

Never under estimate the British!

A German lorry driver in a pub in Newcastle is gobbing off how lazy British truck drivers are.

He's bragging that he drives his load from Hamburg, goes through Holland, Belgium up to Newcastle and back to Hamburg in just two days.

This old Geordie man mutters up, "Ah, way ay I used to pick up me load in Newcastle, drop off in Hamburg and be back in Newcastle for a fish and chip supper the same day".

The gobby German trucker says, "Oh yah, vot rig were you driving then?"

After taking a long swig of his Pint of Newcastle Brown, the old fella replies...

"A LANCASTER BOMBER"

THE WARRANT OFFICER

A cynical old Trooper dies and being of pure heart and clean mind he is instantly transported to the Pearly Gates.

St Peter looks through his personal file and grants the Trooper access to Heaven.

One question says the Trooper

"No bloody warrant officers up here are there?"

"No" Replies St Peter "You're right"

"Good" says the Trooper "I'm not coming in if there is"

No mate, Jobs right, Fill your boots.

For 3 days the Trooper is literally in heaven, free beer, hot water, happy women, and heaven everyday; until! He spots a figure in the distance! Immaculately pressed uniform, the light glistening off his beautiful polished brass, 3 rows of ribbons, steely gaze surveying all around him, pace stick clamped under his tightly muscled left arm and Horror of Horrors on that arm a large coat of arms badge....

The Trooper race's back to St Peter and shouts him up.

"Hey Mate you told me there were no Warrant Officers up here!"

"Yeah! That's right there's none" said St Peter

"Oh Yeah! who's that bloke in the uniform then?" asks the Trooper.

"No mate that's not a Warrant Officer" said St Peter

That's **GOD**....

He just thinks he's a Warrant Officer!

SAS

It's our duty and job to 'stand and stare

Be combat ready and well aware

****

The enemy is close and ready to fight

And here they come walking slowly into sight

****

They are carrying weapons loaded and at the ready

We slowly bring up our sights and aim real steady

****

The enemy talk and laugh and seem so proud

From our position they are compromised and it's going loud

****

I squeeze the trigger and my Demarco taps and hops

The round hits him square; he looks surprised and drops

****

All hope of surprise has been lost and gained

My weapon spits out lead to deal death and maimed

****

The smell of battle smoke is an acrid wheeze

I carry on selecting targets and my trigger squeeze

****

The sound of the bullets and death melt away

Our job is done here; quiet descends and poppies sway

****

We only came here to 'stand and stare'

But you have made us come and death to share.

****

Am I a Crust? (Dedicated to a Veterinarian)

Do you really think I came down the Thames on a crust?

When you look down your nose at me with disdain and disgust

****

I know more about life then university obviously taught you

I've been cold, wet, shot at, bombed and hated; but you in my shoe...

****

...would have probably run, ducked and found somewhere to hide

Sat in a corner; frightened, sucked your thumb and cried

****

I've been in savage war's and nearly lost my limbs and life

Where you have wondered whether to wear the tie picked by your wife

****

So next time you try to lie and pull the wool over my eyes

And tell me my dog is the one licking fur from its thighs

****

Just remember I may not be as bright and as learned as you

But I sure as hell would love you for 5 minutes in my shoe

****

So rip me off and take my money and the Mickey if you must

But just remember 'I Know' and didn't float down on a crust

****

Comments from War Rhymes 1

Poems from Oil Fields to Poppy Fields

****

Sgt Dale Parish

A book from a soldier for a soldier

Those that know; know

AAC Helicopter Rear Crewman

PC Nigel Rousell

It's Awesome

SDUK Trainer

WO1 David Martin-Nash

(Nasher)

Out Fucking Standing!

So proud of you

SAS

PS Garry B

Makes you think doesn't it?

A great insight into the experiences

And thoughts of a veteran, it really hits home – in a good way!

Well done mark!

Charity Co-Founder

Blaine

I just knew you were brave

But some of those poems are legendary

So big salute to you!

Radio London DJ

Comments from War Rhymes II

Poems from the Front Line

****

Graham

War Rhymes 1 was moving

The latest book War Rhymes ll

Has a real feeling of what it must have been like on the front line.

A great achievement Mark and I cannot wait to read your next book

Old Sweaters Club

Darren

Once again Mark has outdone himself

Like the first book thoroughly enjoyed this read

A real insight into the times

Pavement Pounder

Stuart

War Rhymes II

Gives us even more from the 'front line' then the original War Rhymes

Mark poetically offers us a deep understanding of his and other soldiers thoughts as they combat the enemy in harsh conditions armed only with their rifles and a sense that what they are doing is right.

Thank you Mark and more please.

The Upton Grey Nomad

Nasher

Just finished reading Marks second book of poems.

This book flows from page to page.

You can see how he has improved in the short time he has

Put pen to paper and brought his thoughts and memories to

The forefront of literature.

I cannot wait for the release of book 3!

It better be good or I will bitch slap the Muffa Fucker!

SAS (Saturday and Sundays)

Nigel

"Bloody good read"

Honest and refreshing

But you are fucking crazy

Said with huge smile on my face!

Ex Police Dog Handler

Comments from War Rhymes III

Poems for the Politically Incorrect

****

Garry

I have just finished reading books 2 and 3

And I am very impressed!

You are growing as a writer and what you have portrayed is;

At one moment, sad and hard to bear and then;

Like the sun breaking behind a cloud, funny and heart-warming

Thank you for sharing mate!

A Serving Police Officer

Nigel

Mark; War Rhymes lll

And accurate portrayal of our messed up society

This should be a 'must read' for all politicians

Looking forward to number 4

Retired to Devon ☺

Comments from War Rhymes IV

The Collection

****

Graham Raphael

Another interesting book

An accurate and well thought-out

Portrayal of a country in turmoil

Well done!

Nigel R

A great read; yet again I am amazed

You have actually put a sentence together

Without the word Fuck in it!

Retired to Devon ☺

Comments from 28 Days Later

A Veterans Battle against COVID 19

****

Jim O'Dwyer

Mark; just finished the book

Great read mate

The Holt Lane Hobo!

Locky

Mark; just read your book and I must say

Never have you said anything more sensible

Then the Afterword!

Forest Gump

Graham

Another interesting book Mark

Very political, honest and to the point

I loved your comments about social distancing

Might be worth sending a copy to Boris, cheers!

Old Sweaters Club

Comments from
A Veteran in Voice and Verse

****

Leachy

Thanks for your book mate

Loving what I have read so far!

Hope to see you soon mate

A Combat Veteran

A Very Classy Lady

Mark

Having read your rhymes, my feelings were of outrage that the brave members of the SAS dont gets more acknowledgements from the government. I'm sure The majority of the public are similar to me in that they have very little knowledge of the awfulness of belonging to that Company.

On reading the words, your honesty, sincerety, sadness, and your love for your comrades, shone through

The rhymes are very poignant, in fact some of them moved me to tears, and to all of you brave men and women who give your health, and sometimes your lives to keep the rest of us safe. I can only say a sincere Thank you (two very small words, but they have a wealth of meaning.)

Grace

Thank you Grace X

The Old House at Home

OldHouse NewnhamGreen
13 February at 13:44 · 🌐

If you are looking for a good read, I highly recommend this by one of our locals, Mark Lanchbery. It is humorous, eye-opening and heart tugging. Well done Mark, thoroughly enjoyed it.

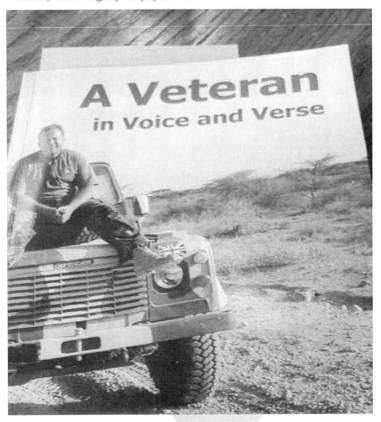

Kind words indeed Thank you

Afterword

During my time a soldier I've been to most of the shitholes around the world; sometimes fighting, sometimes delivering humanitarian aid, sometimes just being there to keep the peace.

I think I have just about seen, smelt, heard and tasted everything;
I have had the misfortune to live and fight alongside incompetent soldiers and inept and downright dangerous officers of our great British Army.

I have also had the privilege and honour to meet and serve alongside some of the most bravest and heroic; hardest men; some of which you would think would never fight, but surprise the hell out of you when the bullets start flying.

I have stood side by side with them when I thought I was going to die, when all I wanted to do was run or hide, but the thing that kept me standing there waiting for my life to go over and out; was the fear of something greater; greater than the fear of dying.

This was the fear of letting my brothers in battle and my friends down, the fear of not standing with them against a baying mob out to kill us; or facing incoming fire so close you could taste the brick dust from the bullets hitting the wall beside your head.

Fear is a strange thing; my way of dealing with fear was to laugh and make light of a harrowing situation, this was not a brave act but a nervous reaction to being close to death.

Some years later when I found myself lying in hospital injured; the lads came to visit with the usual plethora of quality street, crisps, porn magazines, newspapers and of course strong lager, which they consumed in front of me until it was all finished then they would up and leave ☺ on one such occasion they told me in the bad situations we found ourselves in they all used to look across at me to see if I was laughing, if the answer was affirmative they just shrugged and thought to themselves if he is laughing we must be okay and carried on with the fight.

Of course I told them this was not the case I was laughing out of fear, they went away from the hospital that day probably thinking of all the times we had been in the shit and survived.

One of the things that struck me about being in a war zone was the smell; the smell of death, the stink, the flies, the bodies, the body parts, the detritus of war strewn everywhere around the battlefield or contact area.

Those smells come back to haunt me today, every now and then I catch a waft of something that smells similar and it sparks a reaction in me, memories good and bad come flooding back, thoughts and situations again take over my brain and body during the daylight hours and at night the nightmares.

I think out of all the things about going to war and facing death these memories are the ones that take over your entire being, even if it is just for a short time, for that moment you are back there re-living every single moment.

Some go to war for their country, some for the adventure and some because they watched too many war films when they were a kid!

I went to war because I watched those planes crash into the twin towers and was outraged, I couldn't stand by and watch people be murdered, I felt insulted, angry, frustrated and had to do something about it, that very act instilled a sense of injustice that I and many more like me had to somehow put right, some of us again put our lives on the line for what we thought was right.

I re-joined the army to make a difference; to even up the score, to defend my family, and to help to keep our country safe from the people who would want to harm it, once I was actually there and fighting that idealism faded and it became a battle for survival, there is nothing more primeval than wanting to stay alive, wanting to see the next sunset or the next sunrise, once you realise that complete strangers who you have never met actually want to kill you, fighting for survival takes over every rational thought in your mind.

It's when you come home you realise the real cost of your 'little' adventures, the broken relationships, never ending nightmares, the inability to fit in, and back into society, the mates you once had not really knowing the person you have now become, the feeling that what you did was all for nothing, the feeling that the long hard battles fought there; mean nothing here.

The treatment of our veterans is criminally abysmal; I was at an Army Rehabilitation Centre back in 2009 standing next to a group of administration personnel in the smoking shelter with some other wounded servicemen, we were dressed in track suits so they didn't realise we were on a rehabilitation course, when one of the administration staff said to the other, "I cannot stand doing things for these wounded fucking layabouts, I fuck them up whenever I can, I fuck about with their paperwork and pay to make life as difficult as I can for them" the other staff agreed with this 'soldier' and if this was being outwardly said one really does have to wonder what was being unsaid.

****

273

After the Afterword

At times I suffer from anxiety and depression and I do get embarrassed of it and it's not a good place to be in.

I tend to over react to situations, I cannot stop myself from doing this; it's like something takes over, a sort of default mode, even feeling slightly threatened or uncomfortable makes me go from zero to a million miles an hour, sometimes unfortunately people get trampled and hurt in this emotional and physical flat out to the top, if you have witnessed this or been part of it then please accept my apologies.

People don't believe me when I tell them I am suffering because all they see is me being always happy and laughing around them, going further and trying to make others laugh but at times I do struggle, I can be hard to live with or be around when I get this way and I know it!

I try my best to control it and most of the time I succeed, I manage to get on top of it and bite my tongue before hurtful things are said but at times I break, so if you see me and I am quiet or don't speak I am not upset with you nor have you upset me and I also do not mean to be rude, I may just need a minute to myself or a hug.

So please if you are my friend just bear with me I will come back around and probably be funnier than ever, I do feel that things are getting better especially with people like you around me, you give me strength to get through my problems and my mood swings so if your reading this and understanding where I am coming from, I don't need you to say anything or give me your opinion, I just need you to get the beers in ☺

A civilian once asked me why did you call that stranger a brother when you don't even know who he is.
Fair question well presented ☺ well if you notice that stranger is wearing a uniform of the British Armed Forces and that in itself makes us brothers, I don't care where they are from or what colour they are; they my brother or sister because they chose to put themselves second and their country first.

For all I know they have walked where I have walked, left sweat where I left sweat and left drops of blood where I too left drops of blood and that too makes us brothers.

From the time they swore the oath of allegiance and signed on the dotted line until time no longer exists they will forever be my brother, they have my back and I have theirs, we are a family, first and foremost a forever family.

A word on the average NHS worker, the NHS staff do not want or need this bloody ridiculous and completely un-British imbecilic display of false emotion. Ask them, go on! If you want to play 'impress the neighbours' paint your fence or get a new door.

If you want to support the NHS, socially isolate and don't spread corona virus to give them the best chance of keeping infection rates under control. Whether you think it's a real problem or not, that is what they want you to do, so go and order some shopping on line to save a trip out and give yourself a pat on the back; in private.

The last thing any overworked and knackered nurse or doctor needs is deranged people stood on their doorstep clapping or banging pans disturbing their sleep patterns and upsetting their pets.

Fucking grow up and stop being so selfish with your completely unrequested and unappreciated false fucking virtue signalling, it's not what we do, its utterly bloody cringe worthy and its certainly not British.

Sent to me by a frontline NHS worker for inclusion.

****

Afterwar

We come home, we try to fit back in to society, and then the realisation dawns that we are living amongst **some** of the most unsympathetic, uncaring, selfish, self centred, drama queens that **some** of our so called Great British people have turned out to be, but saying that I've met some of the complete opposite to this, one thing I have learnt is we are all different, we come from different walks of life and that is what makes us who we are, but that does not mean we can be intolerant of each other or try to put our feelings and beliefs forcefully onto another person.

I try to think where all this hate and intolerance could have come from? Where did it all start? And how long has it been going on?

We live in a country that has no respect for the police, authority or the law itself, from cocky drunk/drug drivers who have a great chance of getting away with it because it's against their rights to be stopped on suspicion, drivers who hit somebody or something and drive away leaving people injured dying or damaged, drivers who are using their mobile phones whilst wandering over the roads white line, drivers who cannot even be bothered to indicate to which direction they 'might' be taking, drivers who hog the middle lane of a motorway because they know there are no longer 'motorway patrols' to catch and fine them, the 40 MPH brigade who drive at 40 MPH whatever the speed of the road, drivers who think it's okay to leave their car on your drive whilst they go to work and are offended when you place a 'polite' notice on their windscreen asking them 'so kindly' not to do it again, drivers who park on pavements so disabled people and kids have to walk in the road, drivers who will park anywhere to save the cost of a car park ticket even though if the traffic wardens were around to enforce proper parking they would incur an £80 fine, drivers who park on zig zag lines outside of a school placing their children and the children of others at risk just because they are late for their Costa coffee and Pilates class.

And then we have the whingers, the hand wringers and the whiners the pretentious wannabe's, the street stabbing heroes who carry knives knowing the police cannot stop and search them without being called a racist, the so called 'gangs', the city no go areas, the; if you tell me **NO** I will claim my human rights have been violated, the parents who spend more time 'parenting' their mobile phones and their Costa coffee then their kids, the

People who think having the door held open for them is going to cost them something, the no eye contact brigade because it makes them feel threatened, the men who are afraid to say good morning to a woman in case they get accused of something, the people who will never admit they are wrong even though they are, the fear that a man cannot be a gentleman anymore as it will offend women's rights,

The people who cannot answer a direct question without starting the sentence with 'so' the people who have the skill to deliver an answer which has nothing to do with the question they were asked, the police not policing just reacting to incidents, the people walking on eggshells afraid to say anything at all to anyone, the MP trying to get off a speeding charge; getting caught and convicted then appealing in the hope that being from a minority will get them off!

The young girls in Rochdale and other towns not being listened to and having to endure years of abuse because the people that were there to protect them didn't want to seem or be accused of being a racist, the people that hide behind their ethnicity to gain advantage, the poor people who don't know if they are a man today or an elephant or gender neutral, the people who have nothing else to be 'different' so choose the latest label no matter how ridiculous it sounds then get their five minutes of fame on television telling the world they are a non gender specific hedge leaf/koala bear/tree frog, but only for today because something else will be 'in' tomorrow, the people who try to change our wonderful country even though they came here because they liked it as it was, the people who went to university to become intelligent but left without **common sense**.

The sad thing is, the surface has only just been scratched the society in this country is breaking down and it's breaking down because of an apathy because of a fear of doing anything in case it offends somebody somewhere; we have lost the ability to tell someone when they are being ridiculous to:

SHUT THE FUCK UP!

We are told we have to be 'politically correct' why? This country prides itself on free speech the fundamental right of anyone anywhere to be able to have their say, people may not agree and that's okay, we can have a debate, a discussion, we may not always come to an conclusion or agree but that's okay as well, what is happening now is that the very people who want those rights are destroying them by pandering to a minority that to be fair to them have not got a fucking clue what they want.

The fact that good people are frightened to have their say in their own so called free and democratic country is an insult to the very things I and my fellow veterans fought for, we were sent by our government to do their dirty work, to put our lives on the line to protect yours so you could continue to live in a safe and democratic country and now you want to dilute and dissolve everything we went to fight for just because of political correctness; perhaps if you had gone to war to fight for the freedoms you enjoy, you wouldn't be in such a rush to start giving them away!.

I have seen my friends killed, blown apart, maimed, some have died in my arms when the last thing they saw was my ugly face and heard was my voice telling them to not die, but they did die; defending and helping you have the freedom to be politically correct.

Life is a very fragile thing and we as soldiers put ours on the line for you; so you can have the right to wake up in the morning and decide to be that elephant or that gender fluid whatever it is, we don't ask for much in return, a little bit of thought when we find ourselves living rough on the streets, a little thought when we are going through a living hell that is PTSD, a little thought when we have to live with our physical injuries, and a little thought when my neighbour slams their front door and I jump out of my skin because I think there's a mortar coming in!

We have been to some pretty grim places during our time in service for **YOUR** country and seen more suffering, pain, famine, poverty, body parts, death, gore and misery to last us a lifetime.

So next time you feel your life isn't worth living, or your going through some 'drama' or other, love island is not up to scratch or Tesco's fridges don't work and in general life is making you feel a bit low and it feels like it's the end of your world, it probably isn't!
If you were a war veteran it could be a lot worse.

And as for me ever being politically correct! **SHUT THE FUCK UP!** ☺ Never!

**"The only thing necessary for the triumph of evil
Is for good men to do nothing"
ML ☺**

Am I a Monster?

Those who fight monsters inevitably change. Because of all that they see and do, they lose their innocence, and a piece of their humanity with it. If they want to survive, they begin to adopt some of the same characteristics as the monsters they fight. It is necessary. They become capable of rage, and extreme violence.

There is a fundamental difference, however.

They keep those monster tendencies locked away in a cage, deep inside. That monster is only allowed out to protect others, to accomplish the mission, to get the job done.....Not for the perverse pleasure that the monsters feel when they harm others. In fact, those monster tendencies cause damage...GUILT, ISOLATION, DEPRESSION and PTSD. There is a cost for visiting violence on others when you are not a monster. Those who do so know one thing...The cost inflicted upon society as a whole is far greater without those who fight monsters. That is why they are willing to make that horrible sacrifice so that others may live peaceably.

Before you judge one of us, remember this...

We witness things that humans aren't meant to see...and we see them repeatedly. We perform the duties that you feel are beneath you. We solve your problems... Often by visiting violence upon others.

We run towards the things that you run away from. We go out to fight what you fear. We stand between you, and the monsters that want to damage you. You want to pretend that they don't exist, but we know better. We do the things that the vast majority are too soft, too weak, and too cowardly to do. Your life is more peaceful.....because of us.

The current political climate in this country holds that there is nothing worth fighting for. Submission is the popular mantra. Warriors are decried, denigrated, and cast as morally inferior. We know how childish, how asinine, and how cowardly that mindset is... We know this...

There **ARE** things worth fighting, and dying for. We know that not every problem can be solved through rational discourse...that some problems can only be solved through the application of force and violence. And, while we do prefer the former....we are perfectly capable of the latter.

We believe that fighting what others fear is honourable, noble, and just....and are willing to pay the price for that deeply held belief. Why? For us, it isn't a choice...

"It is what we are. We are simply built that way."

We are soldiers...

Special Mentions

The Special Air Service

Nasher my Brother

Ashlee Jane Lanchbery

The Patrons of the Old White Hart

Martin and Lynn Hougeuz

The Old Sweaters Club

John Yourston MM MiD

Johnny 'Pretty Boy' Allum

Michelle and Simone Elton

Brian Bosley II PARA

Mushrooms HA

Robert and Veronica Young

Captain Peter Ellis QGM*

The Patrons of the Eight Bells

Major Hugh Martin

Help for Heroes

Ray 'Razor' Cheeseman

Chelsea Chris

Mick the Bastard II PARA

Special Mention to:

Ryan Francis

And all the fantastic team at

Clocbook Printers

For their time, help and dedication in the production of this book

Special Mentions

Rene 'Uncle Albert' RN

Rose and Linda 'The Terrible II'

Marian and Frank Oakley

Dale Parish AAC

Pikey Matt 'A STAB in the Dark'

Dr Alvin 'Bandits' Skinstad

PC Nigel Rousell

Bob 'The Drill' Bennett IJLB

Sgt 'Percy Roach' PARA

Graham Raphael MSE

Dr Andrew Fernando

Charlie Stockdale

Jim O'Dwyer

Derek Gardner

Charlie Riley

Jocky Munroe

Dr Mark Bruce

The Wonderful Emma Willis

Any Insurgents/Terrorists that took a shot at me and missed!

Other book titles on Amazon from the Author:

War Rhymes I

Poems from Oil Fields to Poppy Fields

War Rhymes

Poems from Oil Fields to Poppy Fields

Mark Lanchbery

Other book titles on Amazon from the Author:

War Rhymes II

Poems from the Front Line

War Rhymes II

Poems from the Front Line

Mark Lanchbery

Other book titles on Amazon from the Author:

War Rhymes III

Poems for the Politically Incorrect

Other book titles on Amazon from the Author:

War Rhymes IV

The Collection

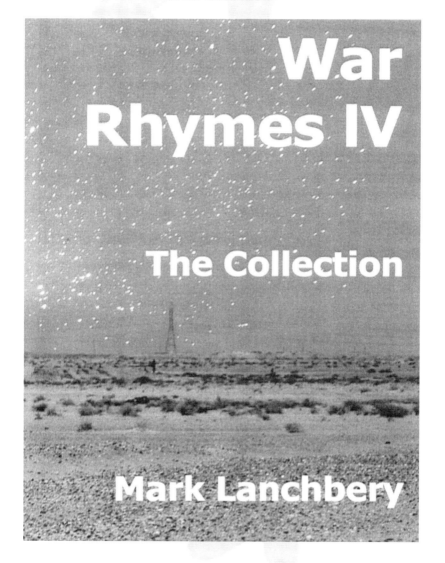

Other book titles on Amazon from the Author:

A Veterans Battle against Covid 19

Other book titles on Amazon from the Author:

A Veteran in Voice and Verse 1st Edition

A Veteran
in Voice and Verse

Mark Lanchbery

Other book titles on Amazon from the Author:

A Veteran in Voice and Verse 2nd Edition

300

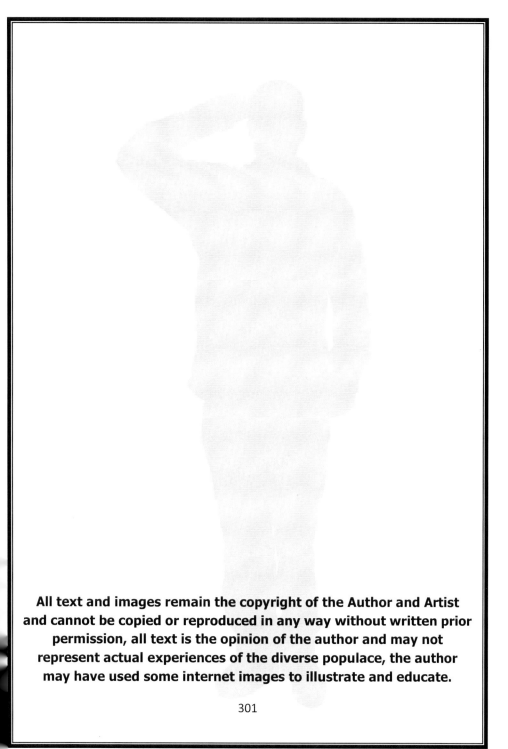

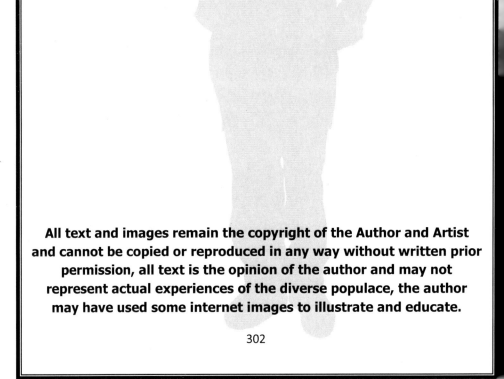